THE MODEL RAILROADER'S GUIDE TO
PASSENGER EQUIPMENT & OPERATION

ANDY SPERANDEO

KALMBACH BOOKS

Acknowledgments

I've learned a lot from others who've shared my interest in passenger trains and passenger operations, and without them this book wouldn't exist. They all have my appreciation and gratitude. Named individually in the photo credits are photographers who have recorded the changing image of the passenger train. Without their efforts and their contributions to Kalmbach's David P. Morgan Library collection, the story of the passenger train would be much harder to tell.

All the passenger train historians listed under "Further reading and reference" have helped to enrich the record of rail travel. Without any desire to slight the others, I'll name Arthur Dubin, Fred Frailey, William Kratville, Tom Madden, Mike Schafer, Joe Welsh, and Pat Wider as among those who have most inspired me.

I offer special thanks to Bill Darnaby, Paul Dolkos, and Kevin Holland, some of whose contributions to *Model Railroader* are republished here. An unfortunately belated thank you goes to the late John Armstrong, whose book *Track Planning for Realistic Operation* has a lot to say about modeling passenger operations. I owe so much to David Barrow, but here specifically for the opportunity to model a prototypical passenger service on his HO scale Cat Mountain & Santa Fe Ry. Thanks, David.

As for what a model railroader can do to represent a great railroad's passenger service, I know of no better example than Chuck Hitchcock and his old Santa Fe Argentine Division layout. Thank you, Chuck, for all the information and inspiration.

Finally, thank you to my friend Mike Shepard, who accompanied me on many jaunts to New Orleans Union Passenger Terminal and helped me begin to understand what I saw there. Together we experienced the twilight of the great trains, in Fred Frailey's phrase, and weren't we lucky to be there. – *Andy Sperandeo*

© 2006 Andy Sperandeo. All rights reserved. This book may not be reproduced in part or in whole without the written permission of the publisher, except in the case of brief quotations used in reviews. Published by Kalmbach Publishing Co., 21027 Crossroads Circle, Waukesha, WI 53186.

Printed in the United States of America

06 07 08 09 10 11 12 13 14   10 9 8 7 6 5 4 3 2 1

Visit our Web site at
http://kalmbachbooks.com
Secure online ordering available

ISBN 0-89024-620-3
Publisher's Cataloging-In-Publication Data

ISBN 10: 0-89024-620-3
ISBN 13: 978-0-89024-620-3

Editor: Melanie Buellesbach
Managing Art Director: Michael Soliday
Art Director: Thomas Ford
Book Layout: Kristine Brightman

CONTENTS

Introduction: **Passenger trains over the years** — 4

Chapter One: **Types of passenger trains** — 7

Chapter Two: **Passenger train equipment** — 25

Chapter Three: **Passenger train consists** — 44

Chapter Four: **Prototype consists** — 52

Chapter Five: **Stations and terminals** — 68

Chapter Six: **Passenger operations** — 81

Appendix: **Further reading and references Manufacturers and suppliers** — 94

Passsenger trains over the years

INTRODUCTION

As a young railfan, one of the author's favorite trainwatching spots was the station throat at New Orleans Union Passenger Terminal. In this afternoon view along Earhart Blvd., the Southern Pacific's *Sunset Limited* from Los Angeles recently has arrived. A few tracks over, the Illinois Central's *Panama Limited* waits to depart for Chicago at 4:30 p.m. *James G. LaVake photo*

When I was growing up, passenger trains occupied a much larger place than they do now both in the world of railroading and in the public consciousness. Eight mainline railroads served my hometown, New Orleans, when I was in high school, and seven of them ran passenger trains into the city. Before I could drive, I often pedaled my bike to New Orleans Union Passenger Terminal in the afternoon to watch the 4:30 departure of the Illinois Central's *Panama Limited* to Chicago. I could enjoy the "sailing" of this magnificent orange-and-brown streamliner and easily make it home in time for dinner. It should probably go without saying that the *Panama* always left on time.

Looking back, hanging around NOUPT in those days gave me a good basic introduction to passenger railroading. The *Panama* always ran with a perfectly matched set of cars, finished off with a classic "boat-tailed" observation car, but that was true of few other trains I saw in the late 1950s and the 1960s. Several of the roads serving our terminal mixed heavyweight steel cars with newer streamlined lightweights. In some cases the heavyweights had been "modernized" and disguised with streamliner paint schemes, but six-wheeled trucks and higher rooflines usually gave them away. Cars from "foreign" railroads – any line other than the seven using the terminal – were common. The Railway Express Agency had its own fleet of express refrigerator cars, but most railroads put "RAILWAY EXPRESS AGENCY" lettering on their baggage cars too, and they used them even more for express shipments than for passengers' baggage. The terminal had its own diesel switchers and a lot for them to do. It was free entertainment for a young railfan and model railroader, but also instructive.

With that kind of background, it's understandable that I'd appreciate the interest and enjoyment that passenger trains can add to model railroads. And now more than at any other time in the development of the model railroad hobby, we have the wherewithal in terms of cars, locomotives, structures, and accessories to do true justice to real-life passenger trains and their operations. This book is an effort to give you the background to know what to do with all the great passenger-train models on the market today.

In the chapters that follow, you can learn about the different types of passenger trains and their varied missions, and decide what kinds of passenger trains to include on your own railroad. There's an even greater variety in types of passenger cars, and the explanations of them will allow you to determine the appropriate cars for your railroad and its trains. Cars tend to be arranged in passenger trains in certain well-defined patterns, and when you understand the patterns you can develop your own believable freelanced train consists. Reviewing some examples of prototype (real-life) consists will demonstrate both how you can put together models of specific passenger trains and also the possibilities for

Passenger train time line

1893 – Congress passes the United States Safety Appliances Act requiring air brakes and automatic knuckle couplers on all cars, freight and passenger. Pullman patents the enclosed, full-width vestibule that becomes a de facto standard for passenger cars in the 20th century.

1902 – The vapor system of steam heating is patented for passenger-car application by Egbert H. Gold. Heating with steam supplied by locomotives had been used since the 1880s, but Gold's system provides an even, controllable steam supply throughout the train. Railroads begin a general conversion to vapor steam heating, and the Chicago Car Heating Co., later the Vapor Heating Co., forms in 1904 to exploit Gold's patents.

1905 – The Long Island RR begins the first large-scale use of electric multiple-unit cars in commuter railroad service.

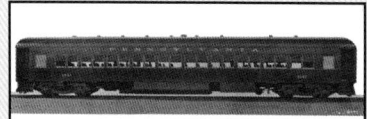
Pennsylvania RR photo

1907 – Beginning of the heavyweight era, when all-steel passenger cars, including the Pennsylvania RR P70 coach and the Pullman 12-section, 1-drawing-room sleeper *Jamestown*, are introduced for safety, especially in the new Hudson River Tunnels leading to New York City's Pennsylvania Station.

1909 – General Electric builds its first production gas-electric passenger railcar. Gas-electrics established themselves as an economical alternative to steam-hauled branchline and local passenger trains. The new Electro-Motive Corp. delivers its first gas-electric car in 1924.

1921 – Following several years of experimentation, the Pennsylvania RR begins installing roller bearings on many passenger cars. The PRR example is followed by the Chicago, Milwaukee, St. Paul & Pacific and the New York, New Haven & Hartford. By 1929 some 850 passenger cars are equipped with roller bearings. The Great Depression slows the wider adoption of roller bearings, but many late-1930s streamliners have them. After World War II hardly any new passenger cars are constructed with solid bearings.

1929 – Formation of Railway Express Agency, owned by a consortium of railroads. Railway Express moves packaged express shipments mostly on baggage-express cars provided by railroads, but operates its own fleet of express refrigerator cars.

1930 – Carrier air-conditioning goes into regular service on Baltimore & Ohio dining car *Martha Washington*, followed soon by dining car 1418 on the Santa Fe's *Chief*. Railroads and the Pullman Co. begin widespread installation of air-conditioning in older equipment in the mid- to late 1930s. By 1940, 27 percent of U.S. passenger cars are air-conditioned, including all new streamliners.

1933 – The Pullman Co. builds an experimental lightweight sleeper-buffet-observation car, the *George M. Pullman*. Although built of aluminum with a round, enclosed observation end and riding on four-wheel trucks, the car's otherwise conventional riveted construction distinguishes it from the streamliners that followed.

Chicago & North Western Ry. photo

1934 – Beginning of streamliner era. Union Pacific's M-10000 is the first streamlined, lightweight, articulated passenger train with internal-combustion-electric power; the Chicago, Burlington & Quincy's *Zephyr* is the first streamlined, lightweight, articulated passenger train with diesel-electric power.

1936 – The Budd Co. delivers its first full-size streamlined lightweight stainless steel chair car, Atchison, Topeka & Santa Fe 3070. In the same year Pullman builds its first full-size streamlined lightweight non-articulated sleeping car, the 8-section, 2-compartment, 2-double-bedroom *Forward*. In 1937, the streamlined *Super Chief*, built by the Budd Co., is the first lightweight all-sleeping-car train with full-size, non-articulated, individual cars. Lightweight cars initially weigh 30 to 40 percent less than equivalent heavyweights.

5

1944 – Court decision requires Pullman Inc. to divest either its car-building or sleeping-car operations. Pullman retains its car-building arm, Pullman-Standard, and sells sleeping-car operator Pullman Co. to a consortium of railroads. Most Pullman-owned sleeping cars are sold to the railroads using them between 1946 and 1948, and leased back to the Pullman Co. for operation.

Chicago, Burlington & Quincy photo

1945 – The Chicago, Burlington & Quincy places the first bubble-top dome car in service, the rebuilt Budd coach *Silver Dome*. The Burlington also orders new dome cars, to be delivered by Budd in 1947, for its Chicago-Twin Cities *Twin Zephyrs*. Also in 1947, Pullman delivers four dome cars for the General Motors *Train of Tomorrow* demonstration train.

1949 – Budd Co. introduces a modern replacement for the gas-electric, the self-propelled Rail Diesel Car (RDC). Unlike gas-electrics, RDCs offer the flexibility of multiple-unit operation. The first production RDCs are delivered in 1950.

1950 – Commuter railroads begin adopting two-level gallery cars and soon introduce push-pull operation using the multiple-unit controls of diesel-electric locomotives.

1952 – Milwaukee Road purchases the first full-length dome cars from Pullman-Standard. Santa Fe and Great Northern follow by purchasing full-length dome cars from Budd in 1954 and 1955, respectively.

1956 – Santa Fe re-equips its *El Capitan* coach streamliner with double-deck Hi-Level cars and later uses Hi-Levels on other trains as well.

1960 – Grand Trunk Western ends the last regular use of steam locomotives in revenue passenger service on a Class 1 railroad in the United States.

1965 – Kansas City Southern buys the last conventional single-level coaches built for intercity passenger service before Amtrak.

1967 – The United States Post Office cancels almost all Railway Post Office and passenger-train storage mail contracts with the railroads. The loss of this revenue leads to widespread cancellation of already-declining passenger service on freight railroads. REA Inc., the successor to Railway Express Agency, shifts much of its ground transport to trucks and to trailers and containers carried on freight trains.

1969 – Metroliner high-speed electric multiple-unit cars ordered by PRR begin service for Penn Central between New York City and Washington, D.C., in what becomes known as the Northeast Corridor. (The Northeast Corridor was extended to Boston when the New York, New Haven & Hartford was included in Penn Central.)

1971 – Launch of Amtrak national rail passenger service on May 1 allows freight railroads to cancel their remaining passenger trains. Only the Chicago, Rock Island & Pacific; Denver & Rio Grande Western; Long Island RR; and Southern Ry. elect not to join Amtrak and to continue operating their own passenger trains. Rio Grande and Southern were obligated under the legislation creating Amtrak to continue their passenger operations through 1974; commuter-oriented LIRR is still carrying passengers.

George Drury photo

1973 – Amtrak receives its first new passenger cars, Amfleet equipment built by Budd with tubular Metroliner-like carbodies and inside-bearing Pioneer III trucks. The new cars introduce all-electric head-end-power (HEP), which becomes Amtrak's standard. Amtrak begins converting its Heritage Fleet second-hand equipment for HEP operation.

1980 – Amtrak introduces Superliner double-deck passenger cars by Pullman-Standard for long-distance service outside the Northeast. These are the last passenger cars built by P-S, and a later order of Superliners will be built by Morrison-Knudson.

2000 – Amtrak introduces *Acela Express* tilting-body high-speed trains for Northeast Corridor service on December 11. *Acela* trains are powered by electric locomotives at both ends for bi-directional operation.

There was a lot of fascinating detail to take in along the passenger platforms at NOUPT. At the right in this view is a Santa Fe lightweight sleeper that will go to Oakland, Calif., by way of the Missouri Pacific as far as Houston, Texas. A couple of tracks over, a heavyweight Pullman sleeper is still in service. *James G. LaVake photo*

freelance operations. Understanding stations as the many-faceted hubs of passenger service can help you adapt their varieties to many model railroad situations. Finally, you'll find suggestions on how to put your passenger trains through their paces as if they really carry people, mail, and express. The operation on your model railroad is the key to long-lasting enjoyment of these trains.

Any book can only be an introduction to such a broad and fascinating subject. For a general historical background, I've included a time line of significant passenger train developments centered around the 20th century. If you're interested in learning more, there's a list of references and further reading to take you deeper into the subject. And since I can only scratch the surface of the passenger modeling marketplace, a list of manufacturers and suppliers will help you find what's available in all the popular modeling scales.

There's still a lot of kid in any model railroader, and in a sense I'm still that kid on the bike across the tracks from NOUPT's Clara Street interlocking tower. If in this book I can communicate some of that kid's enthusiasm, along with some of the knowledge he's accumulated in the many years since he watched the *Panama Limited* pull out, I think you're in for a lot of fun.

– *Andy Sperandeo*

Types of passenger trains

There are many types of passenger trains and many different ways of describing them. I'll list and explain a variety of types, but remember that not all of the types are mutually exclusive, and that these are general descriptions with many specific variations.

The *Tulsan*, train 212 on the Atchison, Topeka & Santa Fe, arrives at Kansas City on Chuck Hitchcock's HO scale Santa Fe Argentine Division layout. Number 212 will terminate here after making a daylight run from Oklahoma, but its last chair car and its parlor-observation will continue to Chicago on no. 12, the *Chicagoan*, from Dallas. *Chuck Hitchcock photo*

With a long consist including many express and mail cars, the Atlantic Coast Line's *Everglades* was a classic example of an accommodation train. It made numerous local stops and handled much of the online station work to allow more prestigious through trains to run on faster schedules. The southbound train is shown leaving Broad Street Station in Richmond, Va., in 1951. *Bill Taub photo*

Accommodation trains were the secondary maids of all work that allowed the flagship limiteds on the same route to make fewer stops and thus maintain faster schedules. Accommodation trains typically carried a mix of coaches and sleepers along with plenty of mail and express "head-end" business. In some cases they retained older heavyweight equipment after the railroad's flagship had been streamlined; this was the case with the Illinois Central's Chicago-New Orleans *Louisianne*. Or a road that was upgrading its premier train might use its older lightweights to add class to an accommodation train, as the Northern Pacific did for its St. Paul-Seattle *Mainstreeter*.

Commuter trains taking workers into and out of large cities might be the passenger trains most familiar to the largest segment of the public. Commuter operations feature frequent trains operating on short headways (little time between trains) during the morning and evening rush periods, with service lulls at midday and overnight.

Train schedules offer the challenge and variety of all-stops locals sharing tracks with expresses that pause only at the busiest stations. Several branches to outlying communities might merge through interlocked junctions to form a multiple-track trunk line into a big-city station.

With steam and early diesel operations, it was necessary to have a means of turning engines or complete trains quickly at termi-

◀ Commuter trains gained a distinctive look in the 1950s when high-capacity double-deck gallery cars began to replace single-level heavyweight coaches. The Chicago & North Western had its new Pullman-Standard gallery cars equipped for push-pull operation with diesel locomotives. Here a cab car complete with headlights, horns, bell, and pilot leads an inbound commuter train; the diesel on the other end of the train will lead on the outbound trip. *C&NW photo*

nals. When electric multiple-unit cars were introduced in the early twentieth century, they eliminated the turning requirement and allowed terminals to be much simpler. Modern diesel push-pull trains, which can be controlled either from the locomotive on one end or from a special passenger-carrying cab car at the other, share this advantage.

Modern commuter railroads operated by state and municipal authorities add colorful variety to a rail scene dominated by a few giant freight systems.

Day trains were timed to leave their originating terminals and arrive at their end points in the daytime, or at least without requiring overnight travel. These trains might have all-coach or all-chair car consists, but often also included parlor cars for first-class passengers. Among the well-known day trains were the Southern Pacific's *Daylights* between Los Angeles and San Francisco, the Milwaukee Road's *Hiawathas* between Chicago and the Twin

The Southern Pacific's *Daylight* was an aptly named fast day train between San Francisco and Los Angeles. Its handsome GS-class 4-8-4 locomotives and brilliant red-and-orange paint scheme made it memorable. This is train no. 99, the *Morning Daylight* to San Francisco, at Chatsworth, Calif., on October 29, 1941. *R.H. Kindig photo*

For daytime service between Washington, D.C., and New York City, the Pennsylvania RR offered the streamlined *Congressional*, equipped with stainless steel Budd chair and parlor cars. Operating on the PRR's multitrack electrified main line behind GG-1 locomotives, the trains made speedy morning and afternoon trips in both directions. This is a morning *Congressional* at Fairmount Park, Pa., on December 17, 1952. *David G. Knox photo*

Bound for Ashland, Wis., on Lake Superior, the Chicago, St. Paul, Minneapolis & Omaha's local train no. 508 was photographed as it left Minneapolis on August 4, 1950. The train's consist suggests that its mission involved considerably more express and mail than passenger traffic. *Bob Borcherding photo*

Locomotive-hauled local passenger trains were expensive to operate, making them prime targets for the economies of self-propelled gas-electric cars. This is the Minneapolis & St. Louis local from Albia, Iowa, to the Twin Cities, photographed at Mason City, Iowa, with a wood-sheathed coach providing the passenger accommodation while the gas-electric car itself carries the mail and express business. *Gordon E. Lloyd photo*

Cities, and the Pennsylvania RR's *Congressional* between Washington, D.C., and New York.

Local trains were generally short-distance and typically unnamed runs providing coach, express, and mail service to every station along a portion of a railroad. On three smaller Appalachian coal roads – the Clinchfield, the Virginian, and the Western Maryland – mainline locals provided the only passenger service. On bigger roads, locals often plied branch lines to carry traffic to and from mainline stations. In the 1920s and 1930s, these branchline locals were often converted to gas-electric operation to lower crew and equipment costs. Or a major passenger carrier might offer mainline local service in an especially populous region, as the Santa Fe did on two mainline routes across the Los Angeles Basin between downtown L.A. and San Bernardino.

Long-distance trains included those requiring more than 24 hours between their end points. Such trains most often carried both coaches or chair cars and sleeping cars, such as the Southern Pacific's *Sunset Limited* between New Orleans and Los Angeles. There were famous all-Pullman long-distance trains too, such as the Santa Fe's *Chief* between Chicago and Los Angeles. The premier long-distance trains usually had fast schedules for the shortest possible travel time, but accommodation trains covering the same route would be slower to serve more communities along the way. Some long-distance trains were operated primarily for vacationers, with slower schedules designed for enjoyment of the scenery. The term "cruise train" was sometimes used for such trains, and the best-known example was probably the *California Zephyr* streamliner, also described below under "Pool trains."

Mail and express trains were common in the times when parcel post and the Railway Express Agency were the primary package delivery services. Certain lines with more mail and express traffic than could be handled on regular passenger trains operated dedicated schedules for what was quite a profitable business. The Pennsylvania RR and New York Central both had several unnamed mail and express trains, while other roads gave them descriptive and evocative names like the Burlington's *Fast Mail* between Chicago and Omaha and the Santa Fe's *Fast Mail Express* between Chicago and Los Angeles. Mail train consists included Railway Post Office and mail storage cars, baggage cars in express service, and express box and refrigerator cars. They might or might not have limited coach accommodations for passengers, but they would always have some kind of rider car for the train

The *Chief* of the Atchison, Topeka & Santa Fe was a great example of a long-distance train. Inaugurated as an all-Pullman luxury service between Chicago and Los Angeles in 1927, trains 19 and 20 were given streamlined lightweight equipment (except for Railway Post Office cars) in 1938. The *Chief* wasn't regularly dieselized until after World War II, however, leading to scenes of unstreamlined steam power such as 4-8-4 no. 3781 climbing the east side of Cajon Pass with no. 19's stainless-clad consist. *F.J. Peterson photo*

The Santa Fe's aptly named *Fast Mail Express* was less than 200 miles from its terminal in Los Angeles when photographed at West Victorville, Calif., in 1950. The mail train's 14-car consist is heavy with baggage-express, express, and mail storage cars, but it also includes a Railway Post Office car. A baggage-coach combine brought up the rear as a rider car for the train crew and deadheading railroaders; after 1942 the *Fast Mail Express* wasn't advertised to carry passengers. The train in the background is the eastbound *Chief*. *Stan Kistler photo*

◀ A New York, Ontario & Western 2-8-0 Consolidation hauls a variety of milk cars and an open-platform wood-sheathed combine at an unknown location. Some milk cars resembled express reefers but actually had glass-lined tanks inside. Others were flatcars carrying either permanent or removable milk tanks. *H.R. Edsall photo*

crew. Rider cars also carried railroaders "deadheading" to their next assignments. A rider car might be an older coach or combine, but the Pennsylvania RR had special cabooses designated as rider cars for mail trains.

Milk trains were a specialized kind of local particularly prevalent in New England, the Northeast, and the Midwest. In general they operated from rural terminals into big cities, picking up dairy traffic by the carload and in less-than-carload lots, with a coach or two for passengers. Outbound runs would distribute cars for the next day's loads. Despite many stops, inbound milk trains often had to maintain tight schedules as part of an intricate dairy delivery system.

Mixed trains were the lowliest form of passenger service, a combined passenger and freight run used when traffic couldn't support a separate passenger schedule. The most typical mixed train equipment was a baggage-coach combine (combination car) tacked on behind the string of

From practically the earliest days of railroading, mixed trains carrying both passengers and freight were used to serve lines and stations that didn't generate enough traffic to support separate passenger trains. That was the case on the Milwaukee Road's branch line between Janesville and Mineral Point in southwestern Wisconsin. Here in the summer of 1952 is the eastbound mixed made up and ready to leave at Mineral Point's historic stone depot. A heavyweight baggage-coach combine, a pair of covered hoppers, and a bay-window caboose are behind the venerable Ten-Wheeler. *Paul E. Larson photo*

◀ Overnight trains were scheduled to get passengers between their end points with only one night spent on board. Most carried both coaches and sleeping cars, but often the coaches were "chair cars" with individual reclining seats to provide a little more comfort in the economy price range. Here's the Chicago, Rock Island & Pacific's *Rocky Mountain Rocket* rounding a curve at Bureau, Ill., on its trajectory from Chicago to Denver. The unusual second diesel unit is an Electro-Motive AB6 with a cab in its blunt forward end. The special unit was split off at Limon, Colo., with a *Rocket* section to Colorado Springs. *Ira H. Eigsti photo*

freight cars and often also serving as the train's caboose. The ride would be rough and slow, and the crew might do whatever freight switching work was required at each station before spotting the combine at the depot to let passengers get on and off. You might associate this kind of operation with short lines in bucolic settings, and you'd be correct. Big railroads also used mixed trains, however, to serve their less-important branch lines. Class 1 mixed-train operators included the Atchison, Topeka & Santa Fe; the Chicago, Milwaukee, St. Paul & Pacific; the Great Northern; the Norfolk & Western; and the Union Pacific. On a major railroad, a mixed train might traverse part of a busy main line to reach the junction with the branch line that it would take to its service terminal.

Overnight trains left their starting points in the late afternoon or early evening and arrived at their end points the next morning. Often these were all-Pullman or all-sleeping-car trains. Famous examples included the New York Central's *20th Century Limited* between Chicago and New York, the Pennsylvania RR's *Broadway Limited* between the same cities, and the Illinois Central's *Panama Limited* between Chicago and New Orleans.

Pool trains were operated by two or more railroads between their end points, usually with each carrier contributing part of the equipment. Perhaps the best known of these was the *California Zephyr*, the post-World War II Chicago-Oakland streamliner jointly operated by the Chicago, Burlington & Quincy; the Denver & Rio Grande Western; and the Western Pacific. A famous pool train in the Southeast was the New York-New Orleans *Crescent*, a joint operation of the Pennsylvania RR, Southern Ry., West Point Route, and Louisville &

▲ *Auto-Train* was operated by a private company over the lines of the Richmond, Fredericksburg & Potomac and the Seaboard Coast Line railroads between Lorton, Va., and Sanford, Fla., near Orlando. In the 1970s and 1980s, it allowed travelers driving from the northeastern United States to Florida to take their cars with them on the train and spend the night aboard instead of driving through or stopping at a motel. The trains featured sleeping cars, dome coaches, and full-dome lounge cars. The three 3,600-hp General Electric U36B locomotives were needed to handle the lengthy *Auto-Train* consists. *Victor Hand photo*

▼ Behind the passenger cars each *Auto-Train* included several enclosed double-deck auto carriers for the passengers' vehicles. The trains' operating crews rode in extra-tall cabooses with wide cupolas. Altogether this *Auto-Train*, southbound near Petersburg, Va., on May 26, 1979, had 47 cars behind its trio of U-Boats, and the photographer estimated its speed to be more than 65 mph. *Curt Tillotson Jr. photo*

Nashville. Pool trains might consist of matching equipment in a consistent color scheme, as with the *CZ* and the Chicago & North Western/Union Pacific/Southern Pacific *Streamliner City of San Francisco*, but a train like the Southern Ry./Norfolk & Western *Pelican* between Washington, D.C., and New Orleans was made up of lightweight and heavyweight cars wearing both the Southern's stainless steel and Pullman Green liveries, as well as N&W Tuscan Red.

◀ The *California Zephyr*, a pool train made up of matching stainless steel Budd equipment, carried the markings of owners CB&Q, D&RGW, and WP. It replaced the *Exposition Flyer* in 1949 and featured then-new Vista-Dome cars. Domes gave passengers spectacular views of Western mountain scenery and weren't bad for viewing the Chicago skyline either. The F3s are backing the *California Zephyr* toward Chicago Union Station on August 21, 1950. (*Model Railroader* photo by Wallace W. Abbey)

Modeling opportunities

Here's an example in HO scale of a commuter train that operates on freight railroad tracks. New Mexico *Rail Runner* trains serve Albuquerque on former lines of the BNSF Ry. These are Athearn models of Bombardier gallery cars and an F59PH diesel in *Rail Runner's* striking paint scheme. *Andy Sperandeo photo*

Big-city commuters: Your modern, freight-only carrier might not be part of Amtrak's route structure, but it's obliged to allow trackage rights for the local rail transit authority's commuter trains. With short push-pull consists, today's commuter trains don't require a lot of layout space for stations or terminals.

Double-duty consists: Arrange staging tracks so that your overnight train can drop its sleeping cars in staging and operate as a day train during daylight hours. Back in staging, it can pick up the sleepers again to emerge as the overnight train on another schedule. The rear car of the Pullman section might be a round-end observation; the day train might end with the dining car, which can have a portable signal light hung on its tailgate, where it will be hidden by the diaphragms when the sleepers are coupled on.

Extra sections with steam: Your forward-thinking railroad may have dieselized its regular passenger trains, but summer tour trains (contracted by tour operators and using off-line sleeping cars), fall football specials, and the Christmas mail rush can all justify pulling some of those modern 4-8-4s back from the extra freight pool and using them in passenger service one last time. "Next year" your road will have more E units or passenger-equipped GP9s, but for now enjoy the variety that led you to model the "transition era" in the first place.

Favorite-prototype pool train: Run a pool train sharing cars from a prototype railroad you like but that you aren't modeling on your layout. It will add variety and give you a good reason to have passenger cars from one or more railroads. If the cars are a different type and color than the home road's, so much the better – the differences will make the train's connections with the wider transportation network more obvious.

Milk-train switching: Run milk trains to add passenger switching action if your part of the rail system doesn't justify setting out and picking up Pullmans or head-end cars. Your way freights can be involved too, spotting empties left on station house tracks by outbound milk runs at the dairies and placing loaded milk cars at the station for easier pickup by the inbound milk train.

Mixed on the main: Operate a mixed train from your online terminal into the closest staging yard to represent a branch line that you don't actually model. Besides the passenger interest, the "notional" branch line becomes another destination for freight traffic that will need to be sorted out in your freight yard.

Steam passenger locomotives

The 4-6-2 Pacific type was the most common steam passenger locomotive in North America. The Missouri-Kansas-Texas no. 399, shown here at St. Louis in 1946, is one of the largest passenger steamers on the "Katy." *Bruce R. Meyer collection*

Mountain was the most common name used for the 4-8-2 type, and such eight-coupled engines were first built for more pulling power than Pacifics on mountain grades. Modernized Missouri Pacific no. 5323 was at St. Louis in 1939. *Louis A. Marre collection*

Passenger steamers were generally distinguished by four-wheel lead engine trucks and large-diameter drive wheels. Both attributes were concessions to speed over drawbar pull. The four-wheel lead truck offers better guidance through curves and turnouts, but at the cost of one less pair of drive wheels than a freight engine of comparable weight. With large drivers, an engine travels farther for each piston stroke, and the rotating speed of the rods and valve gear is lower for any given track speed. However, larger drivers sacrifice torque for starting and low-speed lugging.

Since passenger trains are typically much lighter and shorter than freight trains, these compromises made sense for locomotives built to pull them. Terms such as "large drivers" may be relative to a railroad's grade profile. Flatter roads might consider 79" or 80" drivers "large," but carriers with difficult grades might see 70"- or 73"-diameter wheels as large enough. (In comparison, for much of the steam era, wheels of 57" to 63" diameter were typical for freight engines, and only in the last decades of steam's development were 69" or 70" drivers widely used on freight power.)

Some smaller details characteristic of steam passenger locomotives were train steam connections at the rear of the tender and air-whistle communication hoses on both the tender and pilot.

The locomotive supplied steam to the train for heating and hot water; railroads that used steam-ejector air conditioning (the Atchison, Topeka & Santa Fe; Chicago, Milwaukee, St. Paul & Pacific; and the Erie) also used locomotive steam in those systems. The insulated metal steam pipes had swiveling joints at right angles for the required flexibility at couplings.

Signal lines, connected through the train by an extra air hose at each coupling, allowed the conductor to signal the engineer by blowing an air whistle in the cab. Locomotives used in dual service – freight and passenger – were also

continued on page 16

continued from page 15

Horsepower for greater speed was the reason for a four-wheel trailing truck supporting a larger firebox. That made the 4-6-4 Hudson type the logical next step from the Pacific. The New York Central introduced the type in 1927 and amassed a roster of 275 Hudsons. This is J-1 class no. 5220 leaving Buffalo Union Station with a mail train for Cleveland. *H.W. Pontin photo*

The ultimate steam passenger power was the 4-8-4 Northern type, introduced by the Northern Pacific in 1927 and named for that railroad. Number 2682 was a member of class A-5 built by Baldwin in 1943, completing the NP's roster of 49 Northerns. It's shown at Missoula, Mont., on April 25, 1946, with a passenger extra. *R.V. Nixon photo*

equipped with these connections, as were many freight locomotives to make them available for extra or standby passenger service.

By the 1920s, most steam locomotives had steam-powered turbogenerators for electric lighting and sometimes signal equipment. Some engines used in commuter service had either a second generator or a larger generator with greater capacity to supply electricity to commuter coaches not equipped with axle-driven generators. These locomotives also usually sported large conduits running the length of the boiler and tender with sockets for the cables that carried power to the train. Unlike modern head-end-power (HEP) connections, these sockets were usually at the top of the commuter coach vestibules.

From the early 20th century almost to the close of steam operation, the most common wheel arrangement in passenger service was the 4-6-2 Pacific type. When these engines became outmoded for mainline limiteds, there were often still many secondary, branchline, and commuter trains for them to haul. Roughly concurrent with the Pacific, the 4-8-2 Mountain type offered additional capacity for steeper grades and the heaviest passenger trains. Many 4-8-2s were built for freight service too, and this wheel arrangement was well-suited to a dual-service role.

In 1927 both the 4-6-4 Hudson and the 4-8-4 Northern (to use the most common of this wheel arrangement's many names) brought the advantages of higher horsepower to passenger operations. Their four-wheel trailing trucks supported larger fireboxes, giving them greater steam-generating capacity. That translated directly into an increased ability to do work at speed: horsepower.

Of the two types, the Hudson was the most purely a passenger locomotive and saw little freight service. Although 4-6-4s were built for a number of railroads, only the New York Central, which introduced and named the type, acquired a really large fleet of Hudsons. Some of the biggest 4-6-4s were built for the Chicago & North Western, the Milwaukee Road, and the Santa Fe. All three roads' big Hudsons had 84" drivers under high-pressure boilers with large fireboxes and were among the fastest steam locomotives ever. Effective as the Hudsons were, the early introduction of diesel-electric passenger locomotives limited both their application and their service lives.

The Northern could be almost as fast as the Hudson and was not only effective in a passenger role, but became the most widely used dual-service type since the 4-4-0 American Standard of the 19th century. Railroads from coast to coast developed significant fleets of 4-8-4s, although a number of them were built primarily for freight service. On many roads they represented the ultimate development of steam power.

Large articulated locomotives were rare in passenger service, except for two Western railroads faced with both tough grades and long-distance runs. The Southern Pacific used its simple articulated 4-8-8-2 Cab-Forward locomotives on many heavy passenger trains. The Cab-Forwards climbed mountains without the helpers or double-heading that might be needed even with 4-8-2s and 4-8-4s. With 63" drivers, they weren't speedsters, but the SP employed them on runs where their power was more valuable than speed.

The Union Pacific assigned its 4-6-6-4 Challenger simple articulateds to passenger trains on its lines to the Pacific Northwest and to Southern California. These modern engines had 69" drivers and were designed to be smooth and steady riders at speed. The Challengers could easily maintain the schedules of all UP passenger trains except the fast Streamliners.

The last steam passenger engines in regular revenue service were retired in 1960.

Diesel passenger locomotives

The diesel-electric locomotive achieved its first road-service successes on passenger trains in the mid to late 1930s. In those early days of diesel development, even relatively progressive railroad managements had doubts about whether the new power was up to the demands of freight service. However, they could see that early diesels had sufficient capacity for passenger trains, especially with the new streamlined lightweight equipment. In passenger service, small numbers of the expensive new locomotives could make a significant impact, and their promise of lower operating cost was attractive to companies earning most of their revenue carrying freight.

Publicity was an important value too. Despite steam-powered lightweight trains, the terms "diesel" and "streamliner" were effectively married in the public's imagination. For these and other reasons, many railroads concentrated on "dieselizing" their passenger trains before their road freight operations. (The diesel's advantages in switching service were apparent from the very first, so steam yard switchers were also early targets for replacement.)

From the late 1930s through the 1960s, the most common diesel passenger locomotive was the E unit built by General

The most widely used passenger diesels from the late 1930s through the 1960s were the Electro-Motive E units, twin-engine locomotives with four traction motors on two six-wheel trucks. This photo at Memphis, Tenn., in August 1952 shows how the standardized locomotives were customized with paint schemes for individual railroads. Illinois Central no. 4000 is a 2,000-hp E7; St. Louis-San Francisco 2022 is a 2,250-hp E8. *Champion* is one of the racehorse names the Frisco gave to its racy red-and-gold E units. *James G. La Vake photo*

Motors' Electro-Motive Division. In standardized versions from the EA through E9, these were streamlined carbody locomotives with twin diesel-generator sets inside. They rode on two six-wheel trucks with four traction motors on the outboard axles – an A1A-A1A wheel arrangement.

Some Western roads and others with challenging grades deployed freight diesels like the EMD F units in passenger service, with all the locomotives' weight riding on powered axles in a B-B wheel arrangement – two four-wheel trucks, all axles powered. This was less of a stretch than using steam freight engines in passenger service, as the relative speed of diesel locomotives with equivalent horsepower is largely governed by the gear ratio between the traction motor and the driving axle. With different gearing, the same unit can be either a lugger or a diesel speedster.

Other builders offered similar types but trailed EMD in market share. The most successful competitor was the Alco-GE PA and PB series, A1A-A1A carbody units with single turbocharged diesel engines driving robust General Electric generators and traction motors. In a few cases, roads that were late in dieselizing their passenger trains, including the Delaware & Hudson, Grand Trunk Western, and Norfolk &

continued on page 18

continued from page 17

Amtrak's most successful locomotives of the 1970s and 1980s were the Electro-Motive F40PH model, 3,000-hp cowl units riding on two-axle, two-motor GP-type trucks. Auxiliary alternators provided electric hotel-power for Amtrak's new fleet of head-end-power-equipped passenger cars. Amtrak 373 and a sister unit are at Seattle in June 1984. *Andy Sperandeo photo*

Amtrak introduced the General Electric Genesis type P42 diesel in 1993. With 4,200 hp and up-to-date electronic systems, the four-motor GE units haul passengers on all non-electrified parts of the national system. Some units are even equipped to take electrical power from the third rail south from Harmon, N.Y., into New York City's Grand Central Terminal. These Genesis units were at Los Angeles Union Passenger Terminal in the summer of 2005. *Andy Sperandeo photo*

Western, used hood-type B-B diesel road switchers as their primary or sole passenger power. Hood units were also widely used in commuter services and secondary mainline passenger trains. Mechanically, the diesel locomotive worked equally well in any kind of body.

By the late 1960s, the passenger diesels built in the 1940s and early 1950s were wearing out. But with North American rail passenger service also in decline, there wasn't much of a market for new passenger locomotives. Some carriers went for basic freight-type hood units equipped with steam generators and faster gearing, such as the GE U28CG and the EMD SDP40 and SDP45.

However, led by the Santa Fe, a few roads showed enough interest in replacing or supplementing their older power to inspire a new version of the passenger diesel. The "cowl unit" offered an enclosed carbody – the cowl – on the underframe and running gear of a conventional hood diesel (for ready conversion to freight service when passenger trains expired). Unlike the bridge-truss carbodies of earlier cab units, the cowl wasn't structural but only an enclosure.

The first to take the rails, in 1967, was the GE U30CG, a cowled version of the 3,000-hp U30C freight diesel. Quickly after came the Electro-Motive FP45, a cowled adaptation of the 3,600-hp SD45. The Santa Fe bought examples of both types, decking them out in its red and silver warbonnet livery. The Great Northern and the Milwaukee Road also bought small numbers of FP45s. These first cowl units were hardly streamlined, though the rounded nose and roof of the U30CG made more of a nod in that direction than the angular, boxy FP45.

In preparation for Amtrak's inauguration in 1971, the cowl unit owners did indeed re-gear them and reassign them to freight service. But then Amtrak turned out to be a pretty good customer for cowled diesels. The 3,000-hp F40PH, for several years the standard Amtrak locomotive across the United States, is a B-B cowl unit. As regional and local transit authorities were organized to reinvigorate or create new commuter rail service, they also adopted cowl units.

The major exception to this trend is Amtrak's current first-line power, the GE P42 Genesis locomotive. Though these B-B units may look little like the old Es and Fs, their monocoque bodies are structural supports and not mere cowlings.

In pre-Amtrak times, a defining feature of the passenger or dual-service diesel was its steam generator, an automatic, oil-fired boiler that produced steam for heating (and in some cases air-conditioning) passenger cars. Its external details include stacks and vents in a roof hatch, usually at the rear of carbody units and in the high nose of earlier hood units. When F units were adapted for passenger service, the steam generators were typically carried in the booster or B units, with the space at the rear of the cab or A unit used for a water tank. The FP7 and FP9 passenger variants had extended bodies to make room for a water tank, so they could operate without boosters when one unit was sufficient for a train.

Electro-Motive GP7s and GP9s equipped for passenger service often had their air-brake reservoirs on the roof to make room for an underbelly water tank, producing what railfans dubbed the "torpedo-boat" variation (after the resemblance of the rooftop tanks to torpedo tubes on World War II PT boats).

A major element of Amtrak's modernization program in the 1970s was to convert its inherited equipment to electric "hotel power" for heating and air-conditioning as well as lighting. Instead of coming from axle-driven generators on each car, this electricity is now supplied from the locomotive, using either an auxiliary alternator driven by the main diesel engine or a separate engine-generator set. The outward details of head-end-power or HEP-equipped locomotives are receptacles and electrical cables to carry current to the train. As mentioned in the sidebar on steam passenger power, HEP was adopted by commuter carriers well before the formation of Amtrak in 1971.

Self-propelled cars

Self-propelled passenger cars offer railroads a cost-saving alternative to locomotive-hauled passenger trains. Double-ended cars don't have to be turned at terminals, saving both time and the expense of building and maintaining balloon tracks, a turntable, or wyes. Several types of self-propelled cars have been used on American railroads.

Gas-electric cars. These most often resembled combination cars with a cab and engine compartment added to the baggage end. They used gasoline engines (later distillate-fueled and diesel engines) to power electric generators driving traction motors geared to the axles of the lead truck. In terms of this "electric transmission," they were the forerunners of diesel-electric locomotives. In fact, diesel pioneer Electro-Motive got started in the railroad business by building gas-electric cars in the 1920s. A few early gas-electric cars were built with wooden bodies, but most of them were built in the 1910s and 1920s with riveted steel bodies, though generally of lighter construction than conventional "heavyweight" passenger cars.

Gas-electrics, also known by the popular nickname of "doodlebugs," were cheaper to operate than steam-hauled trains, in part because they could get by with smaller crews. They could be built in almost any configuration, but the baggage-coach combine and similar combines, including small Railway Post Office apartments, were the most popular. Such cars could operate as one-car trains serving lightly trafficked branch lines or in mainline local service. Some doodlebugs could pull a lightweight trailer car or two, or a few freight cars for mixed-train service.

After World War II the need for the kinds of services gas-electrics could offer fell off sharply, and even where there was traffic, the old cars were becoming obsolete. The last regular gas-electric passenger services came to an end in the early 1960s.

Electric multiple-unit cars. As railroad electrification got started in the late 19th century, multiple-unit controls allowing one operator to drive several coupled power cars were an early development. The application of such equipment to steam-railroad commuter services grew

The gasoline-electric self-propelled car offered a low-cost alternative to locomotive-hauled trains for branchline and local passenger services. This is Burlington car 9838 running as local train no. 12 at Virden, Ill., on May 29, 1948. It's a one-car train with mail, baggage-express, and passenger compartments. *Gordon Lloyd photo*

The successor to the gas-electric was the Budd Rail Diesel Car or RDC, introduced in 1949. The RDCs came in five versions with different arrangements of passenger, baggage, and mail compartments. Their multiple-unit capability gave the RDCs flexibility and power for quick acceleration and a good turn of speed. The Baltimore & Ohio called its RDCs *Speedliners*. This *Speedliner* train is making a quick stop at Cumberland, Md., in the early 1950s. *B&O photo*

rapidly in the early 20th century, especially in the Northeast, and also in Chicago and San Francisco. These m.u. cars were mostly high-capacity coaches, but there were baggage-coach combines and baggage-mail cars as well. Since every car was powered (sometimes every other car), they offered a relatively good power-to-weight ratio and quick acceleration.

continued on page 20

continued from page 19

Economical, efficient, and bi-directional, m.u. cars outlasted their heavyweight beginnings and began to be built in new lightweight incarnations in the late 1950s and early 1960s. The Pennsylvania RR's high-speed replacements for locomotive-hauled trains in its electrified Northeast Corridor were Budd m.u. cars with tubular bodies called "Metroliners." Today electric m.u. cars are still the principle equipment of commuter services in the Northeast and on lines east and south of Chicago.

Diesel multiple-unit cars. In the early 1950s, the Budd Co. introduced the self-propelled Rail Diesel Car or "RDC." In one sense these cars were the next generation of doodlebugs, but with the important advantage of multiple-unit controls, just as on electric and diesel locomotives and electric m.u. cars. They were also double-ended, a capability rarely developed or exploited in gas-electrics. Since their power plants were compact, under-car packages, their entire carbody length was available for carrying passengers, baggage and express, and mail. The RDC cars were built in several standard configurations and also some customized versions.

An RDC could be a one-car branchline train or a multicar mainline service. They were useful in commuter service and also on intercity runs. Like electric m.u. equipment, an RDC train of several cars could leave a big-city station and split off one or more branchline trains at junctions along its run.

In the early 1980s, with most RDC cars aging or retired, Budd introduced the SPV-2000, an updated replacement vehicle based on the tubular Metroliner body that Amtrak had also adopted for its Amfleet equipment. The rail passenger market had shrunk, and the SPVs never equaled the numbers of their RDC ancestors. They did see service with Amtrak and remain operational with some commuter authorities. The diesel multiple-unit or "DMU" may be in temporary eclipse, but there are proposals and even experimental cars that promise to keep the concept alive.

8 tips for better passenger cars

Reliable performance and realistic appearance

Andy Sperandeo's passenger cars are adjusted for correct height, close coupled, and connected with working diaphragms. And check out the finish on that fluted stainless chair car. *Jim Forbes photos*

Attractive as they are, passenger cars are just a little more trouble than freight cars. That's okay, though, because if you're any kind of a passenger fan at all you know they're worth the extra effort. After years of building and operating passenger car models, I've learned a number of things to do with them that pay off in both added realism and extra reliability. I don't claim to have discovered everything I'll say here on my own. I've been fortunate to learn from some outstanding modelers, and I believe the best way for me to repay them for the knowledge I've gained is to pass it along.

I work in HO scale and some of what I have to say is specific to models and products in that scale.

If you're in another scale you can still aim for the same goals, but you may have to find your own way to get there. And while I'm modeling the time when the old heavyweight steel cars and lightweight streamliners served side by side, a lot of this will apply to the contemporary scene as well.

1 Car height. The height of freight cars can vary tremendously, but passenger car heights were very consistent in late steam/early diesel times. Most heavyweight cars, including the Pullman Co.'s standardized sleepers, measured 14 feet from the rails to the top of the roof. It's important to me to know that Atchison, Topeka & Santa Fe heavyweights were generally about 14'-3" tall, and if your favorite prototype's cars were a different height, by all means use that dimension. Lightweight streamlined cars were, if anything, more standardized, and almost all of them measured 13'-6" over the roof.

You'll find, however, that many models, especially older models in both plastic and brass, ride higher than they should. Most often they were manufactured that way to allow for extra truck swing on sharp model curves. But it's easy to see that full-length 80- or 85-foot HO passenger cars look their best only on curves of 30" radius or even larger.

If you build your layout to that standard, you can let your passenger cars sit down a little lower on their trucks, and the trucks will still have all the

The reworked brass car on the left is the correct height for a Santa Fe heavyweight, 14'-3" over the roof. The car on the right, an almost-stock Rivarossi model, stands too tall.

swing they need. The cars will look better in profile, forming trains of matching height, and individual cars will appear better proportioned and not jacked up off their wheels.

(If you want to model double-decker cars like the Santa Fe's Hi-Levels or the many varieties of bi-level commuter equipment, you're on your own for dimensions. My advice, though, is to learn what height those types of cars should be and adjust your models accordingly.)

2 Modified caliper. If you've already wondered how tall your passenger cars are in scale feet, you've probably discovered that it's not so easy to whip out the typical scale rule and get an accurate measurement from the railhead. You need an instrument adapted to the job, like the caliper shown below.

I made my height-measuring tool from an inexpensive plastic dial caliper modified with Evergreen Scale Models styrene and some 1-72 brass machine screws, nuts, and washers. The dimensions of the added arm aren't critical, but the arm should be long enough to reach the flat top of a clerestory or arched roof past the coupler and diaphragm on the end of the car, and of heavy enough stock to be rigid. It also needs to be square with the bar of the caliper. There's nothing to stop you from fashioning a brass or steel arm and adding it to a higher-quality stainless caliper, but I felt more comfortable using my modest machining skills on plastic and a low-cost tool.

With General Tool's HO scale dial caliper, you can read the height of your cars directly in scale feet and inches. That, compared with the prototype dimensions, will show you exactly how much to lower any car – they almost never need to be raised.

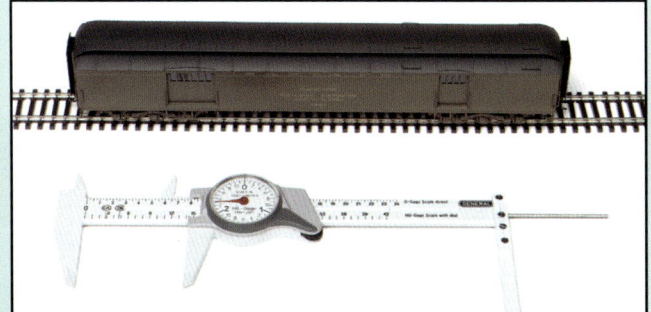

Andy modified this General Tools no. 1401 caliper to make it handier for measuring the height of any rolling stock. To use it, extend the depth gauge rod to rest on one railhead, and slide the bar of the

caliper down until the added arm rests flat on the car's roof. Then you can read HO feet and inches from the caliper's scale and dial. (Modelers in O scale can use General's no. 1405 dial caliper.)

3 Bolsters.

The most effective way to lower a car is usually to modify the body bolster. On plastic cars such as the Rivarossi heavyweights, you can use your caliper as a depth gauge to measure the height of the bolster from the car floor (looking at it upside-down), then subtract the amount you want to take off the car's height to see what the height of the bolster should be.

On the Rivarossi cars, I like to shave off the round boss on the bolster using a no. 17 chisel blade and fill the kingpin hole with a piece of 1/8" plastic tubing long enough to serve as a kingpin or truck-mounting boss. Then I add a square styrene plate of whatever thickness it takes to bring the bolster up to the needed height – laminated from different thicknesses if necessary – with a 1/8" hole to fit over the tubing. The tube can be tapped for a 2-56 machine screw so the truck is easy to remove and replace. The side bearing pins at one end of the car can either be trimmed to the new bolster height or removed entirely.

One other point about the Rivarossi cars: I generally keep their original trucks, which look very good, but replace the wheels. The stock wheels are only 31 scale inches in diameter, but 36" wheels were the standard for almost all passenger cars. You'll need to shave the faces of the molded brake shoes with a no. 11 blade to let the larger wheels turn freely. And remember to account for the effect of larger wheels (36" - 31" = 5", 5" ÷ 2 = 2½") when you decide how high to make the modified body bolster.

To be sure, I don't get the perfect car height every time, but I try to ensure that if I err it's on the low side. I can always add washers to shim the car up – Kadee fiber washers fit over the 1/8" tube – but that won't work in the other direction.

For slightly different approaches that have guided me, see part 2 of Bill Darnaby's article, "Kitbashing heavyweight Pullman cars," in the May 1989 *Model Railroader*, page 104; and John Pryke's article, "Improving HO scale freight and passenger trucks," in the November 1998 MR, page 115.

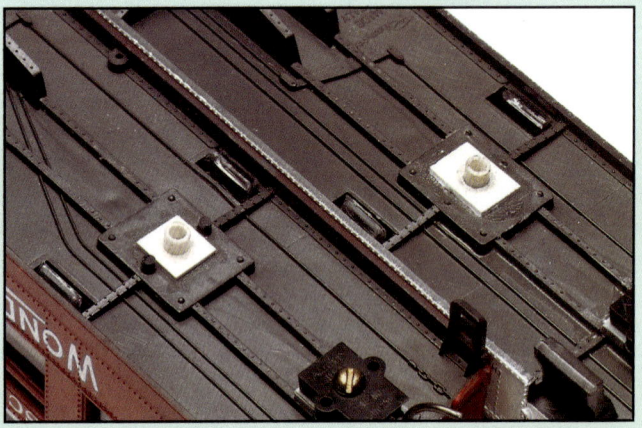

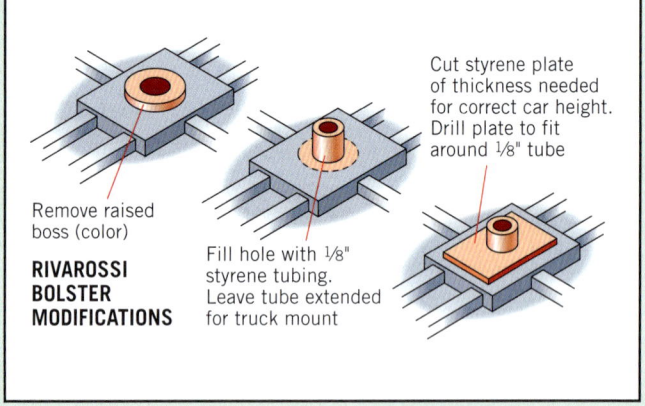

RIVAROSSI BOLSTER MODIFICATIONS

Remove raised boss (color)

Fill hole with 1/8" styrene tubing. Leave tube extended for truck mount

Cut styrene plate of thickness needed for correct car height. Drill plate to fit around 1/8" tube

The bolsters of these Rivarossi heavyweights have been modified as shown in the drawing to lower them to scale height. The 1/8"-diameter kingpin bosses are tapped for 2-56 screws, making it easy to remove and replace the trucks for maintenance and adjustment.

4 Bolsters for brass.

Yes, those expensive imported brass cars can be the wrong height too, though this is more common with older models than with the most recent production. A typical bolster type is a turned plastic button, with a shouldered kingpin screw securing both the truck and the bolster through a nut inside the car. Those nuts are an annoyance, forcing you to unscrew the car floor every time you want to remove or replace the trucks.

So even if the plastic button is the right height, I drill it for the same 1/8" plastic tubing I use on plastic cars and secure the trucks in similar fashion with 2-56 screws. The tubing can be secured in the button with either cyanoacrylate adhesive (CA) or epoxy, and the same adhesives can be used to bond the button to the metal floor.

When the car is too high, though, the button has to go. Then I build new bolsters from thick styrene strips and the now-familiar 1/8" tubing, and screw them to the metal floor with countersunk flathead machine screws. I've learned to mount these bolsters longitudinally in most instances, as that's less

The heavyweight car on the right has its original button bolster, but drilled for a length of 1/8" plastic tubing that can be threaded for a 2-56 screw. The lightweight car on the left has a new bolster built up from styrene strip and tube.

likely to interfere with the trucks as they swivel.

If you'd care to make more realistic bolsters, have at it, but if the car sits down on its trucks as it should the bolsters are all but invisible, even when seen at eye level. I will sometimes add lengths of styrene I-beam or channel to the car floor to simulate the center sill and block any undesirable see-through.

As before, if you're changing wheels or changing trucks, check for differences in wheel diameter and truck bolster height, and take that into account when you make new body bolsters.

By the way, I'm not bashful about using plastic trucks with brass cars, both for better rolling quality and more accurate appearance. I have several models of prewar Pullman-Standard prototypes riding on 43R triple-bolster trucks from D&G Models (P.O. Box 641364, Los Angeles, CA 90064-1364), and prewar Budd-prototype cars with Athearn no. 90411 trucks to represent nine-foot wheelbase 41R trucks. (Cut off the Athearn coupler arms and kingpin bosses, and drill the bolsters out for 1/8" tubing.)

Couplers. I use Kadee no. 5 couplers in their own boxes mounted directly to the carbody. As long as your curves are at least 30" in radius and your turnouts are no. 6 or longer, you can take this simple and direct approach. Forget about mounting couplers on arms connected to the trucks or with long shanks or special boxes for extra swing. This is a lesson I learned from Chuck Hitchcock's old Santa Fe Argentine Division layout, one of the finest examples of passenger train operation I've ever seen. (For more on Chuck's railroad, see his article "Twelve hours at Argentine" in *Model Railroad Planning*, 1997, page 10.)

Chuck also mounted the coupler farther back from the end of the car than you normally see, so the cars couple closer together and the passenger train looks like a tighter unit. On heavyweight cars I follow Chuck's recommendation and drill holes for the mounting screws 3/8" in from the surface where the diaphragm will be mounted. This results in a coupled distance of about 16", very close to scale.

Lightweight cars have square ends without the taper usually found on heavyweights, so this coupling distance may allow the corners of lightweight cars to touch on curves. When I saw that this was happening on my minimum radius, I decreased the coupler setback to 5/16". This makes the coupled distance between lightweights about 20".

To locate couplers consistently, use a simple marking gauge of brass strip bent 90 degrees, with a hole drilled 3/8" or 5/16" from the inside of the bend. I have two gauges, one for each setback.

You can use either a 2-56 screw through the middle of the coupler box or two 00-80 screws in the side ears.

For brass cars I choose whichever screws will let the new holes miss any already drilled in the mounting pad.

Body-mounted Kadee no. 5 couplers make for simple installations and operate reliably. Deep setbacks made consistent by rudimentary brass gauges provide close coupling.

Coupler height. It's important to mount couplers at the correct height and to do it consistently on all cars. Because of their length, passenger cars magnify the chance for unwanted uncouplings when track isn't perfectly level.

Of course, having made the car height accurate I don't want to change that, so to adjust coupler height I move the coupler box up and down, not the car. Down is easiest: Just add shims between the coupler box and the carbody or mounting pad. You can use Kadee's no. 211 coupler box shims or cut your own from thin styrene sheet.

"Up" seemed more challenging until I realized I could make that "down" too. Kadee's no. 27 coupler has the shank offset to the bottom of the coupler head – "underset" in the manufacturer's coinage. That usually turns a too-low mounting into one that's too high – I'm rarely lucky enough for it to be just right – and of course that can be shimmed down.

Sometimes the top of a coupler set back this far will interfere with the end of the car. That can usually be fixed by gripping the coupler's "glad hand" in a vise and filing the glad hand's projection on top of the coupler flush with the coupler head. If the coupler head's rear corner interferes with a mounting pad, as it may on brass cars, I trim the mounting pad with a cutoff wheel in a motor tool.

Passenger cars with no. 5 couplers mounted this way can be reliably backed up a 3 percent grade around a 32"-radius curve, and through no. 6½ turnouts and crossovers.

I know this because my layout is still at a stage where half of all train miles are run in reverse. I should add that I weight my plastic cars to match National Model Railroad Association Recommended Practice 20.1 – about 7 ounces for an 85-footer. The brass cars are all heavier than the NMRA recommends, but I don't worry about that.

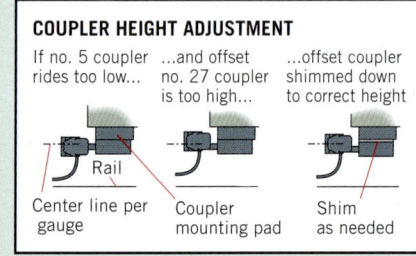

Once car height is correct, adjust coupler height by raising or lowering the coupler box, not the whole carbody. If couplers are too low, the drawing shows how Kadee's no. 27 offset coupler can make adjustments easier.

7 Diaphragms.

These bellows-like connections enclose the space between cars for safe passage through the train. Passenger cars look naked without them, but they can be a pain in the neck if they don't let cars negotiate all kinds of trackwork, or if they keep cars from coupling and uncoupling. Again I took my cue from Chuck Hitchcock, who found reliability in simple modifications he made to an old-line product.

Starting with Walthers no. 933-429 diaphragms, flatten out the folded paper bellows and use a steel rule and a sharp no. 11 blade to trim off one full fold. This lets the diaphragms fit between close-coupled cars. Then fold up the bellows again and rub hard along the folds with the steel rule to reduce their springiness. Chuck called this "taking the fight out of them."

Finally, when assembling the diaphragm, make sure the burr left when the vinyl striker is punched out faces in toward the bellows. You can feel this burr by rubbing a finger across the striker; keeping it on the inside lets the striker slide smoothly against the next one. The sliding strikers let cars move freely though curves and turnouts whether being pushed or pulled.

The modified diaphragms don't interfere with automatic coupling and stay tight on straight track. They will gap open slightly on sharper curves, but otherwise they look good. About the only way to manually uncouple cars with diaphragms is to take slack and pull one glad hand toward you with a wooden skewer. Since that may be possible only on the front track in a station, it's best to plan for magnetic uncoupling.

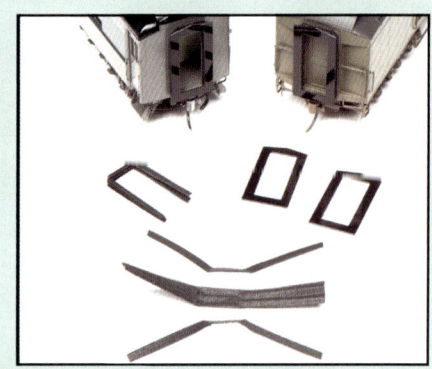

Walthers paper-and-vinyl diaphragms can be modified to make reliable connections between close-coupled cars. Trim one full fold off the bellows (or half a fold off each end as shown here) and mount the striker plate with its burr inside for smooth sliding.

8 Stainless steel finish.

The plastic models of stainless steel cars typically have silver paint that lacks the mirror sheen of real stainless. Even the plated finishes of the brass models don't have a realistic stainless look, and plated cars from different makers don't match.

I hadn't found a finish I really liked, though, until I saw Keith Kohlmann's *Model Railroader* article about painting with Alclad II Chrome lacquer.

First paint the car with a gloss black enamel undercoat. This acts as a background for the mirror-like finish of the Alclad II.

Let the black dry thoroughly, then airbrush the car with the Alclad II Chrome. This lacquer is thin enough to spray without thinning. Be careful not to touch the chrome finish until it's sealed.

Seal the Alclad II with an overspray of Floquil Crystal-Cote or Testor's Metalizer Clear Finish. Then you can handle the model, apply decals as usual, then seal them with another clear coat.

This Lambert brass Santa Fe chair car was made with a plated finish. Painted with Alclad II Chrome lacquer over a gloss black undercoat, it now has a more realistic stainless steel sheen.

Passenger train equipment

Passenger cars were and are built in an almost bewildering variety of configurations and floor plans. When you understand the possibilities, you'll find amazing scope and challenge in modeling them. This chapter will give you an overview of the major types of passenger-train cars.

Passenger cars in a coach yard illustrate some of the variety of different types of equipment. Using them realistically requires understanding their diversity. The scene is on Frank Titman's S scale Spiral Hill RR. *Bob Werre photo*

The most basic passenger car is the coach, represented here by an HO scale model of a New York Central heavyweight steel car built from a kit made by Branchline Trains. The NYC and its subsidiaries acquired hundreds of these cars in the 1920s from several builders, and other railroads copied the Central's design for their own coaches. Model Railroader *photo*

Streamlined lightweight cars were built either with smooth sides or with stainless steel fluting. This HO scale model represents a Budd Co. fluted stainless chair car built shortly after World War II. While other builders added fluted stainless sheathing to carbodies of conventional steel, Budd's carbodies were all stainless steel assembled with a patented welding process. The Walthers model is based on a Seaboard Air Line prototype, though shown here lettered for the Chicago, Burlington & Quincy. Andy Sperandeo *photo*

Here's the interior of a Pennsylvania RR heavyweight coach, from the numerous P70 class. Its floor plan is typical, with bench seats for two passengers each on either side of the center aisle. There are racks above the windows for luggage and rest rooms at either end of the car. Pennsylvania RR *photo*

▲ This Pennsylvania RR P85 chair car model represents a smoothside lightweight car built following World War II. The PRR had tried a two-tone red paint scheme before the war, but in the late 1940s returned to its traditional Tuscan Red paint for smoothside streamlined equipment. The HO scale model is from Centralia Car Shops. Andy Sperandeo *photo*

◀ Lightweight coaches were similar to heavyweights in interior layout, but usually featured lighter colors, larger windows, and better lighting. The rest rooms and adjacent lounges were larger and more comfortable than on older cars as well. Most important to passenger comfort were individual reclining seats, as in this car from the Nashville, Chattanooga & St. Louis streamliner *City of Memphis*. Some railroads referred to cars with these more comfortable seats as chair cars rather than coaches. NC&StL *photo*

Coaches and chair cars

The coach is the most basic of passenger cars, typically with rows of two-abreast seats on either side of a central aisle. Usually there are rest rooms at each end of the car, and there might be a smoking/lounge room adjacent to the men's rest room. An entire car might be designated a smoking car, or a coach could be partitioned with seating for smokers in a third to half of its length.

Coaches for short-distance travel might have closely spaced seats with rigid backs, and some commuter or suburban coaches had 3-2 or even 3-3 seating to pack more riders into each car.

Coaches for long-distance trips would have fewer seats spaced farther apart, and the seats would recline and might even have leg rests for the most comfort possible short of sleeping-car accommodations. The term "chair car" was used by several railroads for their best coaches. Usually a chair car was distinguished by individually reclining seats.

Parlor cars

A step up from the chair car is the parlor car, with individual movable or rotating seats. This was first-class accommodation for day travel, and some parlor cars had an enclosed drawing room offering privacy. Parlor cars might also include a smoking lounge section or bar. On some daylight streamliners consisting mostly of chair cars, the observation car at the rear of the train was the parlor car.

Sleeping cars

The top-line accommodations for overnight and long-distance trains are provided by sleeping cars. From the early 20th century until the streamliner era got going in the late 1930s, almost all sleeping cars in North America were built, owned, and operated by the Pullman Co., founded by George M. Pullman, who developed a nationwide system based on standardized sleeping cars. Pullman Co. cars were so widely known to the traveling public that "Pullman" became the common synonym for sleeping car, and the most luxurious limiteds with only sleeping-car accommodations were often called "all-Pullman trains." (This didn't mean these trains included no other types of cars; in fact they usually had diners and lounges, and often mail and express cars as well. But all-Pullman trains carried only passengers who purchased space in a sleeping car or perhaps a parlor car, and no

The interior of IC car 3351 shows the typical parlor car seating arrangement, with individual revolving armchairs along a central aisle. The porter was on hand to provide first-class service to the passengers. *David P. Morgan Library collection*

The first cars built specifically for Amtrak in the 1970s were the Budd Amfleet equipment, which used the stainless steel tubular body developed for Metroliner multiple-unit cars. Amfleet coaches, riding on inside-bearing Pioneer III trucks, still make up a large part of the Amtrak roster. This HO scale Amfleet coach is by Bachmann. *Andy Sperandeo photo*

Parlor cars provided first-class accommodation for day travelers. This Illinois Central streamlined parlor car, no. 3351, was rebuilt from a 1920s heavyweight. It might look like a lightweight car with its streamlined roof line, but its lineage is revealed by its six-wheel trucks. *David P. Morgan Library collection*

Today's equivalent of the parlor car is the first-class coach on Amtrak's *Acela Express* trains running in the Northeast Corridor. The individual reclining seats are paired as on chair cars, but offer extra legroom, large tray tables, and AC electrical outlets for personal electronics. This is a Bachmann HO model of an *Acela* first-class coach. *Andy Sperandeo photo*

The Pullman Co. made its name synonymous with the sleeping car by both building and operating the overwhelming majority of sleepers on United States railroads in the first half of the 20th century. *Orange County* was one of the most common types, built in 1925 to floor plan 3410A with 12 open sections and one drawing room. This Branchline Trains HO model represents the car as running in the late 1940s, after it was equipped with electro-mechanical air-conditioning in 1935. *Andy Sperandeo photo*

One of the largest groups of lightweight sleeping cars were the 152 plan 4099 cars with six sections, six roomettes, and four bedrooms delivered by Pullman in 1942. *Cimarron Valley* was one of 26 *Valley* cars assigned to Santa Fe service; this Walthers HO model was detailed and painted by the author. *Andy Sperandeo photo*

The 50 Viewliners of 1996 are the replacements for Amtrak's Heritage Fleet conventional-height sleeping cars. Built by Morrison-Knudson, these new sleepers have 12 roomettes, two bedrooms, and one accessible bedroom for mobility-impaired passengers. Viewliners carry both numbers and names with *View* suffixes. This Walthers HO model is lettered as no. 62011, *Gulf View*. *Andy Sperandeo photo*

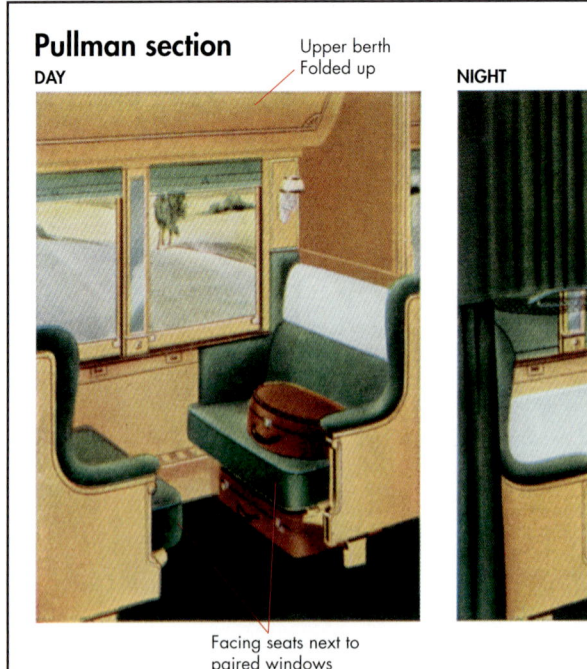

"coach-class" travelers.) See "What happened to the Pullman Co." on page 29.

Sleeping cars are usually described in terms of their accommodations. A very common heavyweight sleeper was the "10-1-2," with ten open sections, one drawing room, and two compartments. A section consisted of two facing seats which made down into a berth at night, and an upper berth that was lowered from the ceiling. Section passengers used community men's and women's lavatories at the ends of the car. A drawing room was a private space with seats and berths for three, and also a private lavatory. Compartments were private rooms sleeping two but with no lavatories.

trains. Far exceeding the number of cars needed for baggage was the portion of the fleet used for express service by the Railway Express Agency.

The Railway Express Agency was formed by the merger of several independent express companies in 1928 and was owned by a consortium of railroads. Until the late 1960s it played the package-express role now occupied by companies such as FedEx and UPS. Many railroads lettered their baggage-express cars "BAGGAGE/ RAILWAY EXPRESS AGENCY" to denote their role in express service. Express shipments included everything from purchases out of the Sears and Montgomery-Ward catalogs to human remains in caskets being taken home for burial.

In addition to running through between terminals, cars in express service might be set out or picked up as needed at stations along a train's route. There were also express messenger cars carrying an onboard clerk to handle shipments at station stops. Messenger cars were equipped with a desk, safe, and toilet for the clerk's use, and beginning in 1948 were required to carry a five-pointed star 6" in diameter for identification.

Express reefers and boxcars.

Special refrigerator cars for passenger-train service date back almost as far as refrigerator cars themselves. The express reefers built from the 1920s into the 1950s were usually about 50 feet long (when most freight cars were 40-footers), rode on trucks suitable for high speeds, and were equipped with passenger-compatible air-brake systems. Air-signal and steam-heat lines passed under the cars for connection between the locomotive and the train, and express reefers typically had buffers above the couplers to contact the buffers in passenger-car diaphragms. The cars were insulated, had tight-sealing plug doors, and had ice bunkers at the ends with rooftop hatches.

In the 1950s, many commuter railroads replaced old single-level coaches with two-level gallery cars. This is a Walthers model of a Pullman-Standard Southern Pacific car used in "commute" service on the San Francisco Peninsula. *Andy Sperandeo photo*

Express reefers carried perishable express shipments such as high-value produce (early harvest berries and melons, for example) and cut flowers. When not needed for perishables, the cars were used in "dry" service (without ice) for any kind of sealed express shipment.

Many milk cars resembled express reefers externally and had similar internal insulation, but in general lacked ice bunkers. Railroad-owned milk cars of this type were occasionally used for express traffic. In other cases the same type of carbody was used to house a pair of large, permanently mounted internal milk tanks, and these cars were not suitable for express loading.

Express boxcars came into widespread use with the steel cars of the 1920s and later. The Pennsylvania RR had the largest fleet, with a significant fraction of its ubiquitous X29-class 40-foot boxcars carrying "RAILWAY EXPRESS AGENCY" lettering. Like express reefers, express boxes also had air-signal and steam-heat connections and passenger-compatible brake systems. Many also had some form of high-speed truck, but were more likely than express reefers to have conventional "three-piece" freight trucks. Three railroads serving the Southeast and Florida – the Atlantic Coast Line, Florida East Coast, and Seaboard Air Line – had express boxcars with ventilators for perishable shipments like melons that might not require insulation.

Express cars of all types, including baggage-express, offer the opportunity to have foreign-road cars (those from another railroad company) appear on our railroads. Besides regular interline connections, express cars leased to Railway Express could show up almost anywhere they were needed.

Commuter cars

The basic car for commuter traffic is the high-capacity coach. For older single-level cars this meant closely spaced seats, often in 3-2 or 3-3 configuration. In the 1950s multilevel cars were introduced to increase seating capacity without increasing train length. Often these were "gallery cars" with the upper seating level open above the main-level aisle. Conductors or ticket-takers can collect tickets or punch passes in one trip through a car, without having to climb up and down. On fast runs with many station stops, this is a significant advantage.

Multiple-unit electric cars were used for commuter service around several large cities. They were controlled from small end cabs, eliminating the need for turning. With the advent of diesel operation, non-electrified commuter services could enjoy some of the same advantages using push-pull consists. Some cars have control cabs for the end of the train opposite the locomotive, and all cars have multiple-unit control cables and air hoses for connections through the train.

Hi-level cars

In 1954, the Santa Fe faced the happy problem of increasing passenger loads on its all-chair car *El Capitan* streamliner. Wanting to avoid consists longer than 14 cars and the expense of regularly operating extra sections, the Santa Fe sought a way to pack more seats into each car without sacrificing the comfort passengers expected on the 2,200-mile run between Chicago and Los Angeles. Taking a cue from multilevel commuter coaches, the road had the Budd Co. build two experimental "Hi-Level" double-deck chair cars.

The Hi-Level cars had a full-length upper deck and a lower-than-normal lower floor slung between the trucks. With center entry vestibules on the lower level, almost the entire upper level could be devoted to comfortable reclining seats for 68, as opposed to the 44 seats of the Santa Fe's newest conventional chair cars. The lower level had plenty of room for baggage stowage, rest rooms and lounges, and a high-capacity air-conditioning system. Stairways at one end of each car allowed the Hi-Levels to be used in trains with conventional equipment. Although it wasn't comparable to the view from a dome, the sightseeing from the wide upper-level windows was better than from single-level cars.

Passengers liked the new cars, and the railroad liked their operating efficiency. The Santa Fe ordered enough Hi-Levels to completely re-equip its *El Capitan* service in 1956.

The new cars came in four types. Full Hi-Level chair cars with straight-through upper floors seated 72 in roomy reclining seats. Each train set also carried two chair cars with stairs at one end, reducing their capacity to 68. A Hi-Level dining

The popularity of the Santa Fe's all-chair-car *El Capitan* Chicago-Los Angeles streamliners gave rise to its Budd Hi-Level equipment. Hi-Level cars afforded greater capacity for a given length of train. Trains *magazine photo by George A. Gloff*

car seated 80 on the upper level, with food prepared in a spacious lower-level galley delivered to the upper floor's pantry by dumbwaiter. Hi-Level lounge cars featured windows curved into the roof line for better views of Western scenery and the Chicago skyline and included a lower-level cocktail lounge where smokers were accommodated.

To give the Hi-Level consist a more streamlined look, the Santa Fe added raised roof fairings at the rear ends of two series of baggage-dormitory combines it had been using on *El Capitan*. These so-called "transition cars" were strictly cosmetic, as the actual steps down to normal floor level were in the front end of the leading Hi-Level chair car. In fact, as the Santa Fe added to its Hi-Level fleet and began using the cars on other trains, it added no transition cars to its roster. Hi-Levels would also operate in the *Chief*, *San Francisco Chief*, *Texas Chief*, and *Grand Canyon*, all without transition cars.

There were no Hi-Level observation cars, so the conversion to double-deck cars meant that *El Capitan* would no longer sport a streamlined stern. However, this move coincided with the railroad's general disenchantment with round-end obs cars.

Even the passenger-oriented Santa Fe had decided that these cars required more special handling than they were worth. At about the same time, the road converted the *Super Chief's Vista*-series observation cars into square-end sleeper-lounge cars for mid-train operation.

The significance of the Hi-Level cars extends beyond the end of Santa Fe passenger service in 1971. As relatively recent, solidly built, and well-maintained high-capacity equipment, the Hi-Level cars were welcomed into the Amtrak roster. There they not only earned their keep but helped to inspire a new generation of long-haul passenger cars, the Amtrak Superliners.

Modeling opportunities

These are ideas primarily for freelance modelers building a passenger roster; prototype modelers have the examples of actual railroads to follow.

Add color to heavyweights: On a railroad making the transition between the heavyweight and streamlined eras, older cars were often painted in streamliner color schemes to blend in with the new lightweight cars. A heavyweight coach or sleeper in streamliner colors will stand out as an extra car added to a normally all-lightweight consist.

Basic car types: Concentrate on buying or building a few basic types of cars, especially coaches, sleeping cars, and baggage-express cars. Similar cars numbered or named in the same series will suggest the existence of a larger fleet than you actually need to model. If possible, have a few extras of these basic cars so you can add cars to regular trains for holidays, run additional sections, and operate specials for big game or tour groups.

Combined "amenity" cars: Use combination car types to add amenities to trains composed of basic cars. A diner-lounge, for example, adds two kinds of service in one car; a dormitory-lounge combines passenger luxury and service-crew accommodations in a single piece of equipment. With such cars you can assemble full-service trains without making consists so long that they overwhelm your layout.

Intercity push-pulls: In the modern era, use push-pull formations for intercity trains to make the most of cramped model facilities. One stub track per train is a good formula for a minimum-space passenger terminal and also for the most economical use of staging track space. (Two push-pull passenger trains might fit on one stub staging track of the same length that you use for freight trains.)

Signature cars for top trains: Save your dome cars and observation cars for your railroad's flagship. These cars can set your finest train apart from ordinary accommodation runs and make it look like something special to your operators and visitors.

Southern Pacific's *San Joaquin Daylights* regularly used heavyweight head-end cars painted streamliner colors in front of otherwise lightweight consists. *Andy Saez photo, Kenneth G. Johnsen collection*

Stick with heavyweight head-end cars: Some roads economized by keeping their heavyweight head-end equipment in service with expensive new lightweight passenger-carrying rolling stock. Lightweight consists with heavyweight head-end cars were commonly seen on roads as different as the Southern Pacific and the Norfolk & Western. (The N&W never owned a lightweight head-end car.)

Modeler's guide to lightweight passenger trucks

by Kevin J. Holland

Passenger car modeling has come a long way in the past decade. The range of affordable, well-executed models, particularly in HO scale, is broad, and passenger car modelers have at their disposal a growing range of accurate detail parts. Related to these developments is a growing awareness of the sometimes subtle variations in passenger car trucks.

Prior to the 1930s, many North American passenger cars rode on six-wheel trucks. While an early motivation may have been redundancy – the failure of one wheel or axle wouldn't, in theory, cause a catastrophic truck failure – six wheels also provided excellent ride qualities and spread

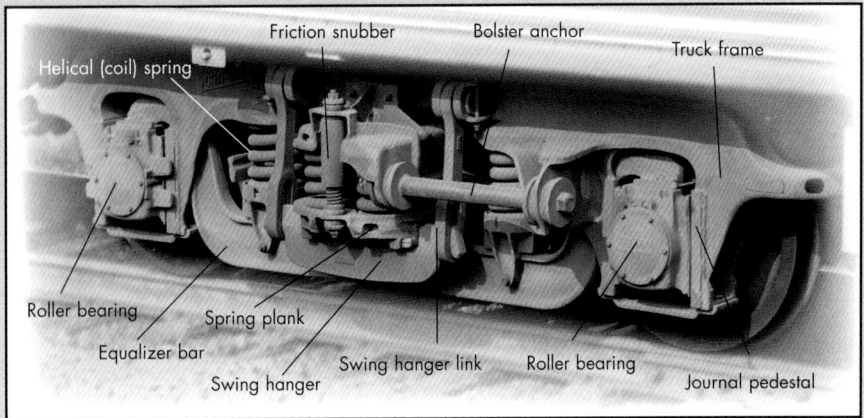

Parts of an outside-swing-hanger truck. *Kevin J. Holland photo*

the considerable weight of later all-steel cars destined to travel over sometimes marginal track and bridges. Cars of this era are termed "heavyweights" for a very good reason!

As the railroads and the Pullman Co. embraced streamlined passenger cars in the mid-1930s, four-wheel trucks were deemed adequate to support the new lightweight cars, eliminating the weight (and cost) of a third wheelset per truck.

Because their "cargo" was less forgiving of bumps, bounces, and jolts, passenger car trucks were more elaborately engineered than their freight-car counterparts [see the December 2003 issue of *Model Railroader* for a guide to freight car trucks. – *Ed*.]. To ensure riders' comfort, designers of passenger car trucks paid particular attention to springing and vertical and lateral stability, in the process developing variations important to modelers.

Many trucks were made by General Steel Castings Co. (GSC), a major supplier of component castings and passenger trucks, several of which were sold under GSC's "Commonwealth" brand. In fact, the term "Commonwealth truck" is widely used in reference to lightweight, four-wheel, drop-equalized passenger car trucks. Although correct when referring to a GSC truck, the Commonwealth name is largely meaningless in identifying specific configurations.

It's possible to group lightweight passenger car trucks into four broad categories. Early trucks were triple-bolster, followed by inside-swing-hanger, outside-swing-hanger, and eventually inside-frame trucks. A typical outside-swing-hanger truck is shown above left.

In the next few pages we'll look at the truck styles likely to be encountered by modelers of the 1935-1975 period.

Kevin J. Holland is a professional writer who specializes in passenger train history and equipment. A long-time model railroader, Kevin lives in Burlington, Ontario, Canada.

Cracking the Pullman code

The Pullman Co., which held a monopoly on sleeping-car service until it lost an antitrust lawsuit in 1944, needed an easy method to describe differences between lightweight trucks on the thousands of Pullman passenger cars. The company developed a simple descriptive system based on the mechanical makeup of a truck.

Some aspects of the Pullman code dealt with details invisible from trackside – such as roll dampers, journal size, and pedestal liner width – that are less important to modelers than they were to Pullman. But the code remains a useful reference because it clearly identifies the difference between trucks that share a common anatomy.

Two numbers led off a typical postwar Pullman code designation: a "4" or "6" to indicate the number of wheels in the truck, followed by a "1," "2," or "3" to denote the number of truck bolsters (1 or 3 bolsters in a 4-wheel truck; 2 bolsters in a 6-wheel truck).

Next in the sequence was a letter identifying the wheelbase: "A" indicated a 7-foot wheelbase; "B," 8-foot; "C," 9-foot; or "N," 8½-foot.

A letter code for journal pedestal-opening width followed: "M" meant a 13⅞" width (favored by the Milwaukee Road); "N" was 13⅜"; and "U" denoted the 14¹⁄₁₆" width favored by the Union Pacific RR. The presence of both elliptical (leaf) and helical (coil) springs was indicated by the letter "P," disk brakes by a "D," roll stabilizers by an "S," and outside swing hangers by an "O." Codes identifying trucks used in articulated connections had the prefix "A."

Typical journal bearings in lightweight passenger car trucks measured 5½" x 10"; the presence of 6" x 11" journal bearings was indicated with an "-11" suffix.

For example, 41-BNO-11 was the Pullman code for a popular postwar configuration: it was a four-wheel, single-bolster truck (41), with an 8-foot wheelbase (B), 13⅜" pedestal openings (N), and outside swing hangers (O). The code indicated the presence of clasp brakes by default; a comparable disk-brake-equipped truck would have included the letter "D" in its designation.

In the Pullman code for prewar trucks, the letter "E" indicated elliptical bolster springs, and an "H" represented the helical bolster springs that were introduced in 1938.

Another new technology, roller bearings, was indicated in prewar Pullman code designations by the letter "R." But that was necessary only when these bearing were a novelty. After the late 1930s, roller bearings were specified in just about all lightweight passenger car trucks and were no longer identified in the Pullman code.

Triple-bolster trucks

Among four-wheel lightweight passenger car trucks, triple-bolster designs offered superior ride characteristics when properly maintained. Needing a responsive suspension for the ultra-lightweight, aluminum-bodied trains on Pullman's drawing board in the early 1930s, designers minimized unsprung weight within the truck, largely through the elimination of equalizer bars. Since each journal was sprung independently – with the springs mounted in flared journal wings – triple-bolster trucks didn't need equalizers. The photo at right shows one of the later triple-bolster configurations, known as the A-43-R.

The earliest use of triple-bolster trucks was under several articulated Pullman-Standard trains: Union Pacific's *M-10001* through *M-10006* and Illinois Central's *Green Diamond*. Most of these early triple-bolster designs were produced by LFM (Locomotive Finished Materials Co.), with GSC entering the market in 1936. A design manufactured by LFM in 1937 for UP (Pullman code U-43-RX) had an unusual truss-like frame and lacked journal wings. Contemporary Budd equipment like the Chicago, Burlington & Quincy's *Zephyr*, with its somewhat heavier stainless steel construction, created fewer truck suspension headaches and therefore could employ simpler single-bolster trucks.

By 1942, mechanical complexity and high maintenance demands spelled an end to the popularity of triple-bolster trucks on new car

Characteristic wings identify this as a prewar triple-bolster truck. This truck is equipped with roller bearings, and its use with an articulated coupling makes it an A-43-R design; it would otherwise be a 43-R. George A. Trager photo

deliveries. Although most users replaced their triple-bolster trucks with single-bolster designs after the war, Southern Pacific, an early adopter, kept some rolling until 1971 – a few of these cars even found their way, briefly, into Amtrak service.

Known to some modelers as "Challenger" trucks – variants having been specified for cars assigned to the 1937 Chicago & North Western-UP-SP *Challenger* – triple-bolster trucks were most notably original equipment on Southern Pacific's prewar *Daylights*, UP's 1937 *City of Los Angeles* and *City of San Francisco*, and on sleeping cars assigned to the 1938 *20th Century Limited*, *Broadway Limited*, *Chief*, and *Super Chief*.

Inside-swing-hanger trucks

The more common single-bolster designs employed a solitary truck bolster, suspended transversely from the truck's one-piece, cast-steel frame by a pair of U-shaped swing hangers. Heavy bolster springs cushioned the car as its weight was transferred from the truck bolster, through the swing hangers, to the truck frame. The car's weight was next transferred through groups of smaller springs to equalizer bars (so named because they equalized the load between the pair of journals and wheels linked by each bar). The ends of the equalizer bars transmitted the car's weight through the journals and wheels to the rail.

Most lightweight car trucks had drop equalizers, shaped like a flattened "U." Single- and double- drop equalizers were used. A photo on the next page shows double-drop equalizers on a 41-R, a common prewar lightweight single-bolster, inside-swing-hanger truck.

Until 1938, elliptical (leaf) springs were used to cushion the truck bolster, and helical springs were employed elsewhere in the truck. Under ideal maintenance and weather conditions, elliptical springs are self-damping – suppressing harmonic action that otherwise could cause undesirable rhythmic motion at speed. Cold temperatures and spotty maintenance could negate this benefit, however, and heavy helical (coil) bolster springs gained favor after their successful use on the Milwaukee Road's 1938 *Hiawatha* and the C&NW's

prewar *400*. The photo below right shows a *Hiawatha* truck. With helical springs employed throughout, several methods were used to deal with the problem of harmonic motion, including snubbers or shock absorbers.

Passenger cars need electricity for lighting and air-conditioning and it was often supplied by axle-driven generators. The truck-mounted generator shown at lower left was used on the 1935 *Hiawatha*. It was driven by a belt from an axle pulley.

Early lightweight trucks had inside-swing-hangers supporting the bolster. Outside-swing-hangers appeared in the mid-1940s. However, inside-swing-hanger trucks continued to be made. The lower right photo shows an inside-swing-hanger 41-CS-11 truck under a 1950 Pullman-Standard car.

This is a prewar 41-R truck with prominent double-drop equalizers, elliptical (leaf) bolster springs, and roller bearings. This truck was frequently used on prewar Budd passenger cars. The double-drop equalizer gradually faded from the scene as builders increasingly favored single-drop designs. *American Car & Foundry photo*

Trucks under Milwaukee Road's 1938 *Hiawathas* were among the earliest to dispense with elliptical springs in favor of helical (coil) springs used in conjunction with damping devices. Undamped, exclusive use of coil springs led to harmonic oscillations that produced an unpleasant ride. *Milwaukee Road photo*

This roller-bearing-equipped truck under one of the Milwaukee Road's 1935 *Hiawatha* cars includes a frame-mounted generator for car lighting. The generator is driven by a belt running from a truck axle pulley a pulley on the inboard end of the generator. Only one generator was required per car. In later years, it was more common to have generators mounted on the carbody, driven by belts or drive shafts. In the postwar era, many cars were equipped with self-contained propane or diesel engine/generator sets. *David P. Morgan Library collection*

Although outside-swing-hanger designs claimed sizeable chunks of the market after World War II, particularly in New England, Canada, and the West, inside-swing-hanger trucks continued to be specified by several large railroads into the early 1950s, including Atchison, Topeka & Santa Fe; Chesapeake & Ohio; Chicago, Burlington & Quincy; New York Central; Pennsylvania RR; and Southern Pacific. This inside-swing-hanger 41-CS-11 truck is under a Santa Fe bar-lounge car built by Pullman-Standard in November 1950. *Pullman-Standard photo*

Outside-swing-hanger trucks

Following experimentation in 1945 on the New York, New Haven & Hartford RR, a highly visible development in passenger car truck design debuted when Pullman-Standard introduced the outside-swing-hanger truck on the 1947 Pullman/General Motors *Train of Tomorrow*. The relocated swing hanger is the "U"-shaped link in the center of the truck (top left photo on next page).

Moving the swing hangers and their springs to the outside of the truck frame dramatically reduced the tendency of passenger cars – especially extra-height dome cars – to rock from side to side. The design change not only improved the ride, it also simplified inspection and maintenance since the relocated swing hanger assemblies were easily accessible. Outside-swing-hangers quickly proved their worth and were used on many passenger cars built from the late 1940s to the early 1960s.

Although four-wheel trucks were generally used during the lightweight era, six-wheel versions of the outside-swing-hanger truck, shown in the top right photo, were developed for full-length dome cars, heavy-duty mail-and-express cars, and other specialized applications.

Bolster anchors appeared in 1939 as a solution to the problem of noise and vibration caused by the truck bolster shifting forward and backward in its seat. As shown in the second photo below, these heavy horizontal bolster anchor rods linked the ends of the truck bolster with the sideframe near one end and typically were oriented toward the car center. Bolster anchors had rubber bushings to further reduce vibration transmitted to the carbody.

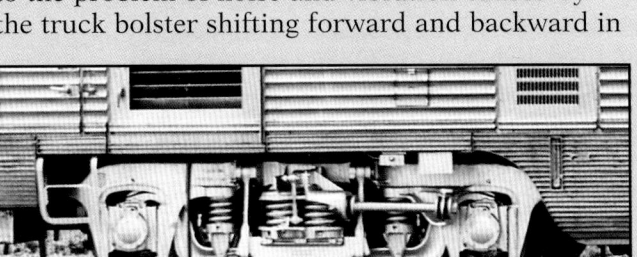

▲ Outside-swing-hangers gained favor in the late 1940s. Santa Fe employed 41-CDO-11 trucks on its Hi-Level *El Capitan* cars of 1956. Budd Co. photo

Top right: Santa Fe's full-length domes rode on six-wheel outside-swing-hanger 62-NO trucks. Budd Co. photo

Right: Horizontal bolster anchor rods began to appear in 1939 as a solution to noise and vibration caused by truck-bolster shifting. David P. Morgan Library collection

Inside-frame trucks

The first ultra-lightweight passenger car truck practical for widespread use was a Budd design introduced on the builder's Pioneer III demonstrator coach of 1956. The radical truck design, shown at right, eliminated swing hangers, equalizers and equalizer springs, sprung journal boxes, and other less-visible components of the traditional truck, reducing weight by roughly two-thirds in the process. About all that remained to support the car and guide the wheelsets were two sideframes, a truck bolster, and two large air springs.

In this ground-breaking design, sometimes referred to as an inboard-bearing truck, the car's weight was transferred through the air springs to the truck bolster and from there by way of side bearings to the sideframes. Placing the sideframes and bearings inboard of the wheels meant a shorter, and therefore lighter, axle.

From trackside, the Pioneer III truck's most distinctive feature was the maintenance-friendly arrangement of its disk brake system, with disks, air cylinders, and calipers mounted outboard of the wheels, as shown in the close-up photo.

With minor variations, the Pioneer III truck format was adopted on many locomotive-hauled passenger cars built in the U.S. and Canada through the 1960s and 1970s.

Budd's Pioneer III inside-frame truck (above) was radical when introduced in 1956, but it paved the way for designs used under later generations of cars. Swing hangers, equalizers, equalizer springs, and other staples of previous truck design were dispensed with. Instead, the carbody was supported on air springs. Bearings were inboard of wheels, and brake disks and calipers, like those on the Canadian National's 1967 Tempo cars, were mounted outside the wheels, as shown in the close-up. Budd Co. photos

The Budd disk brake

The high speeds and frequent stops encountered in lightweight passenger train operation placed heavy demands on brakes and wheels. A stop from 100 mph transfers nearly three times as much energy to the brakes as a stop from 60 mph. Clasp-type brake shoes wore out quickly, wheel tread life was reduced, and so much heat was generated during application that wheels had to be inspected often for evidence of thermal cracking.

Disk brakes solved these costly problems and were first employed on an entire train with the CB&Q's *General Pershing Zephyr* of 1938. The Budd Co.-developed disk brake system found other early applications in Santa Fe's 1938 *El Capitan* and the Milwaukee Road's 1939 *Hiawatha*.

In the Budd system, a ventilated cast-iron rotor, or disk, was bolted to the inner hub of each wheel. Brake pads on each side of the disk were activated by small air cylinders (one per disk). The heat of braking was dissipated by the disks, not the wheels, and wheel tread wear caused by brake shoe friction was eliminated. Budd estimated the life of its disk brake pads at 100,000 miles, versus only 6,000 miles for a clasp brake shoe in the same service, and claimed that ongoing brake pad replacement costs were only about 20 percent of the amount incurred for clasp shoes. Installation of disk brakes, according to Budd, could eliminate as much as a ton of dead weight and require almost 100 fewer major brake-system parts per car.

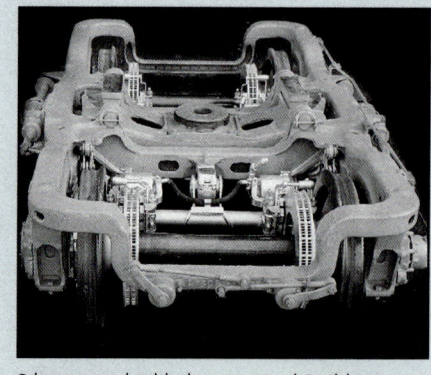

Silver paint highlights a typical Budd disk brake installation on a 41-NDS-11 truck. Fins within the rotors circulate air to dissipate the heat of brake applications. *Budd Co. photo*

Many lightweight passenger cars were retrofitted with disk brakes in the 1950s, and Budd had competition from the ASF Simplex "rotor brake" system.

Since disk brakes mounted inside the truck frame are largely hidden by the wheels, the best spotting feature is the absence of clasp shoes and the attendant brake cylinder mounted on the truck sideframe.

Model trucks

While most ready-to-roll model passenger car trucks feature molded acetal plastic frames, some in HO scale are available as styrene, cast metal, or resin kits, with or without wheelsets. Trucks sold in kit form can give you the flexibility to add or delete certain details – parts like snubbers, shock absorbers, clasp brakes and cylinders, and anti-slide devices – to replicate a specific prototype.

Lightweight passenger cars typically rode on 35", 36", or 36½" wheels. Scale plastic or metal 36" wheelsets are available from several sources. You'll need metal wheels, of course, if you intend to pick up power from the rails to light the interiors of your passenger cars.

N scale passenger car trucks, and most in HO, are rigid. Only a few HO scale offerings are sprung, and then only partially. The fidelity of molded spring detail can vary among rigid model trucks, but molded springs generally yield a heavier, more-realistic appearance than real wire springs.

When present, bolster anchors – the heavy horizontal rod on each sideframe – almost always pointed toward the center of the car; as a result, a bolster-anchor-equipped truck's two sideframes weren't identical. Some older model trucks incorrectly used the same sideframe molding on both sides, making proper orientation of the bolster anchors impossible.

Space precludes a complete list of all available passenger car trucks, but this table gives a sampling of a few of the readily available HO scale versions of the most frequently encountered types of lightweight passenger car trucks.

Suppliers of HO scale passenger trucks
Athearn Trains, 1550 Glenn Curtiss St., Carson, CA 90746

Centralia Car Shops, 1468 Lee St., Des Plaines, IL 60018

Con-Cor, 8101 E. Research Court, Phoenix, AZ 85710

D&G Models, P.O. Box 641364, Los Angeles, CA 90064

Eastern Car Works, P.O. Box L624, Langhorne, PA 19047

IHC, 413 E. Allegheny Ave., Philadelphia, PA 19134

Kato USA Inc., 100 Remington Rd., Schaumburg, IL 60173

Train Station Products, P.O. Box 360, Granville, OH 43023

Wm. K. Walthers, Inc., P.O. Box 3039, Milwaukee, WI 53201

Athearn no. 90411
41-R

Centralia Car Shops CCS4999
41-N-11

Con-Cor no. 97002
41-HR

D&G Models no. P31R
Pullman 43-R triple-bolster

D&G Models no. P61R
1937 UP 43-R-11 triple-bolster

Eastern Car Works no. 9003
41-ER

International Hobby Corp.
No. 4240 41-CN-11

Kato no. 850603
41-D

Train Station Products no. 426
Six-wheel 62-NO

Train Station Products no. 427
Outside-swing-hanger 41-BNO

Walthers no. 1060
GSC-style 41-NDO

Walthers no. 1067
GSC-style 41-HR

Model Railroader magazine photos

HO scale lightweight passenger car trucks

Manufacturer	43-R	41-ER	41-R	41-HR	41-N	41-ND	41-D	41-BNO	41-NDO	62-RDO	62-NO
Athearn			90411								
Con-Cor				97002							
Custom Finishing									310		
D&G Models	P31R										
Eastern Car Works		9003			9009	9002			9007		9023
IHC				4240							
Kato						850603					
Roundhouse					2935						
Train Stn. Products					427/428		427/428	419	414	424/426	
Walthers				1067					1060		

(**Blue** listings indicate metal sideframes.)

HO scale Amtrak trucks (table)

Manufacturer	Superliner 1	Superliner 2	Horizon	Viewliner
Train Station Products	410/411/413	422/423	420	421
Walthers	1046			

Passenger train consists

Train 17 on Bill Darnaby's HO scale Maumee Route is arranged in typical order to form a believable freelanced consist. It's 1955 but the freight-oriented Maumee is still using heavyweight head-end cars. The baggage-Railway Post Office and two baggage-express cars are followed by two lightweight 52-seat coaches and a lightweight 18-roomette sleeper. *Bill Darnaby photo*

THREE

With the many varieties of passenger cars and passenger trains, assembling cars into purposeful and believable consists may seem difficult. There are a few general principles that will help freelance consists make sense, and when you're modeling an actual train you can simply follow the real car arrangement. When you look at the prototype you'll find that there are few hard and fast rules for organizing a train and lots of exceptions. The exceptions can add to the fun when you have a realistic reason to use them on your layout.

Coaches first?

Remember that the coach is the most basic passenger car. Most trains will have one or more. An engine with one or two coaches might be an all-stops local train or an off-peak commuter run. The same engine with five or more coaches could be a rush-hour commuter express or an intercity run between towns an hour or two apart. If you want to put together a special train to a nearby racetrack or ball game, it can be mostly or all coaches.

Though there were and are many examples of trains made up solely of coaches, it's usually more interesting to have other types of cars. It can help to understand how these other cars would be positioned relative to the coaches.

Head-end cars might seem obvious

As the name implies, if a train is to include baggage, mail, or express cars, they would usually go at the front of the train, between the locomotive and the first coach. Express reefers and box express cars might be ahead of baggage cars to maintain a continuous passage to the rest of the train, but not necessarily. Baggage cars in express service would be sealed anyway, and a working Railway Post Office might have access to a storage mail car or two but otherwise would be closed off from the train. Since all the cars have steam and air-signal lines in addition to the train-line air brake pipe, there's no mechanical reason that they can't be in almost any order. (Railway Mail Service contracts usually specified the position and orientation of RPO cars, but these preferences varied a lot on different trains.)

The so-called head-end car or cars might be at the rear of the train. One reason for this could be a terminal where it's inconvenient to turn the whole consist. The railroad would run the locomotive around to the other end of the train, only turning the engine if it's a steamer or single-ended diesel, and leave the train as it is. This became more common during the decline of passenger trains in the late 1950s and 1960s, but wasn't unknown in earlier times.

Another reason could be switching en route. Many Amtrak trains leaving Chicago Union Station used to stop at the nearby coach yard to have express cars coupled on to their rear ends. Some of these trains also set out and picked up express cars along their runs, and the switching could be handled from the rear without interrupting the HEP connections from the locomotive through the passenger cars.

Another exception sometimes seen is a coach, sleeper, or other passenger car mixed in among a group of head-end cars at the front of a train. Usually that's a case of "deadheading," moving a car or cars out of service to some other point where needed or to a car shop for repair or refurbishing. Some railroads called these "DHQ" movements, the abbreviation standing for "deadhead equipment."

Union Pacific train 3, the Omaha-Los Angeles *Utahn* (on the Santa Fe near Victorville, Calif., on May 30, 1950), shows the typical arrangement of a passenger train consist. The four head-end cars behind the Alco diesels include a former Railway Post Office used for storage mail, two baggage-express cars, and baggage-RPO. Then come two coaches; a dining car; a club-lounge-dormitory car; a 6-section, 6-roomette, 4-bedroom lightweight sleeper; and a 12-section, 1-drawing room heavyweight sleeper. The coaches and the 6-6-4 sleeper are through cars from St. Louis via the joint Wabash-UP *City of St. Louis*. Don Sims photo

The starting point for most passenger train consists is the coach, the most basic passenger car. This and the next six photos will show a train built with Pennsylvania RR cars, starting with a Bachmann HO model of a PRR P70 coach. *Andy Sperandeo photo*

It would be perfectly appropriate to add capacity to the basic consist with another P70 coach, but instead we'll use a P85 lightweight chair car. The logic could be that the P85 will be used for long-distance riders, while the P70 carries people getting on and off at intermediate stops. This HO scale car is from a Centralia Car Shops kit and is offered as an assembled model by InterMountain Ry. Co. *Andy Sperandeo photo*

Any sleeping cars on our Pennsylvania RR train will go on the rear. We're showing just one, an 8-section, 1-drawing room, 2-compartment heavyweight car. *Centfaun* is a Walthers HO scale model painted and lettered to represent a sleeping car sold to the PRR in Pullman's 1948 divestiture. *Andy Sperandeo photo*

We'll give passengers on our PRR train food service by placing a dining car between the coaches and the Pullman. That's a typical placement, but not a requirement. This HO scale heavyweight car is a Bachmann model. *Andy Sperandeo photo*

Prototype-minded modelers often say it's better to model the typical rather than the unusual. If you're following that advice, you'll want your head-end cars at the head of the train – most of the time, unless there's a logical reason to put them on the rear.

Sleepers behind the coaches

Unlike the situation aboard airliners, first-class passengers usually rode to the rear of the coaches in "classic-era" – i.e., pre-Amtrak – passenger trains. Usually this meant they didn't have to walk as far from the station concourse to board their cars, and in pre-air-conditioned times it kept them the farthest from the dirty, noisy steam locomotives. If we're talking about a day train, the first-class accommodation may be parlor cars rather than sleepers, but the same considerations usually applied. This sleepers-behind-coaches convention may have been observed more faithfully than any regarding head-end cars, but of course had its share of exceptions.

Consider the case of a train picking up a Pullman in the middle of the night from a station where no switcher was on duty at that time. It might have been most convenient to break the train behind the head-end cars and add the sleeper to the consist ahead of the first coach.

Why pick up a sleeper in the middle of the night? At the height of sleeping car service, many medium-size cities and tourist destinations were served by so-called "setout Pullmans." The car would be set out on a station track in the evening, and passengers could board and go to bed after 9 or 10 at night. The through train they were to travel on would pick up the car when it passed through, and passengers would arrive at their destinations the next morning after a full night's rest. On the return trip, with the Pullman set out at the intermediate stop in the middle of the night, passengers could remain aboard until 7 or 8 the next morning. This is a good excuse for including some passenger-train switching on a layout without having to model a terminal station.

Of course there were those few all-Pullman trains with no coaches for the sleepers to be behind. But those elite trains were exceptions themselves, and many roads didn't have them.

Some Amtrak trains have operated with the sleepers ahead of the coaches for various reasons. In some cases the trains headed into terminals and backed out to depart, so sleepers at the front allowed shorter walks for the first-class trade. In other examples consists aren't turned at terminals, so the sleepers are in front in one direction and behind the coaches in the other. It's also not unusual to see Amtrak long-distance or overnight consists with sleepers at both ends.

Diner in the middle

The most likely place for a dining car in a train including both coaches and sleepers is in between them. Meal seatings can then be arranged to keep the first-class and coach travelers separated, and the coach passengers wouldn't have any reason to pass through the Pullmans.

On an all-coach or all-Pullman train, a dining car might be carried roughly midway in the train so nobody has to walk the length of the train to have a meal. Very long, heavily traveled trains might have more than one diner to handle the large numbers of passengers, and then the dining cars might be spaced apart throughout the train. Or a long train might have a regular diner for the Pullman passengers and a coffee-shop or lunch-counter car for the coach travelers.

In other situations there might be good reason to put the dining car at the rear of the train. The dining car might be set out at an intermediate station after serving dinner. The crew could restock the car and get some rest, then their diner could be picked up to serve breakfast the next morning on a train going the other way. In these cases it might make sense to carry the diner on the rear of both trains, where it could easily be uncoupled and coupled on by a switch engine.

▶ The Southern Ry. *Southerner* was inaugurated as an all-coach streamliner between New York City and New Orleans, with the Pennsylvania RR handling the train north of Washington, D.C. Here its Pullman-built lightweight consist is stretched out on the bridge over Lake Ponchartrain to the east of New Orleans. Behind the E6 diesel are a baggage-dormitory-coach combine, two coaches, a dining car, two more coaches, and a tavern-lounge-observation car. *David P. Morgan Library collection*

A baggage-coach combination car placed ahead of the coaches gives our train more seating for coach passengers and some space for baggage and express shipments. This is the most widely used type of "combine," but there were other variations, such as baggage-lounge and baggage-dormitory-lounge combination cars. Since this train lacks a lounge car, the combine's coach section might be reserved for smokers. *Andy Sperandeo photo*

The combine could probably handle all the checked baggage on our short train, so when we add a baggage car ahead of it we're giving our train greater capacity for express shipments. The baggage car might also carry some storage mail on a run that won't include a Railway Post Office car. This PRR B60b baggage car is a Walthers HO scale model with paint and lettering modified by the author. *Andy Sperandeo photo*

An express refrigerator car, such as this Walthers HO class R50b ahead of the baggage car, gives our train capacity to carry perishable express traffic, maybe shellfish on ice going from a coastal terminal to a market or restaurant in an inland city. But these cars were also used for non-perishable "dry" shipments when their cooling capability wasn't needed. For even more express we could also add an X29 box express car as shown in Chapter Two. All our train needs now is a K4 Pacific or an E7 diesel and it's ready to roll. *Andy Sperandeo photo*

As the first section of an eastbound *Challenger* economy train speeds through Geneva, Ill., the mid-train Chicago & North Western lounge car and diner (third and second cars from the left) flash past. This section of the Los Angeles-Chicago train is made up primarily of tourist sleepers, older Pullman heavyweight cars refurbished to offer sleeping car accommodations at budget prices. *Henry J. McCord photo*

The image of streamlined aerodynamics, a boat-tailed sleeper-lounge-observation car brings up the rear of the Southern Pacific's *Lark* arriving at Los Angeles in December 1947. This all-Pullman train carried only first-class passengers on an overnight run down the SP Coast Line between San Francisco and Los Angeles. *L.O. Merrill photo*

Lounge next to diner

Lounge cars were most often adjacent to dining cars, for many of the same reasons that so many restaurants include bars. The lounge next to a diner gave passengers a convenient place to wait while their tables were readied and encouraged passengers who wanted an after-dinner drink (or smoke) to give up their tables in a busy dining car. If the lounge was behind the diner, these extra luxuries might be reserved for first-class passengers. If the lounge car were a dormitory-lounge combination, the dining car crew would only have a short walk to and from their sleeping quarters and wouldn't have to pass through either the coaches or sleepers.

Major exceptions to placement next to the diner were lounges in cars configured for other purposes. Baggage-lounge combinations, used on many luxury trains of the heavyweight era, were placed either directly behind the locomotive or behind any head-end cars. Observation-lounge cars were clearly meant for use at the rear of a train.

Observation cars

When used, these sight-seeing cars punctuated a train at the rear end. As explained in the last chapter, they were often combinations of more than one car type, such as chair-observations, sleeper-lounge-observations, or cafe-lounge-observations. With an observation car on the rear, cars usually weren't added behind. The observation car, if not the entire train consist, would have to be turned at the terminal. The luxury and eye-appeal of observation cars thus came with operational liabilities.

Popular and attractive as observation cars may be to modelers as well as the general public, the most important thing to understand about them is that all trains didn't have them. In the heavyweight era, many more-utilitarian trains could do very well without them, and in the passenger-train decline of the 1960s, even trains that once rated obs cars lost them. Amtrak used the few observation cars acquired in its Heritage Fleet for several years, but bought no new ones and now doesn't operate any.

The streamliners built between the late 1930s and early 1950s were the last great stand of the observation car, as it seemed that trains with an aerodynamic look needed an ending that at least appeared to enhance airflow.

Still, many streamliner observation cars had relatively square ends, as mentioned in the previous chapter. And it's not hard to find examples of new streamliners created without any observation cars – the *Texas Chief* (1948) and *San Francisco Chief* (1954) on the Santa Fe, and the *Sunset Limited* (1950) on the Southern Pacific.

The switching opportunities with observation cars may not be as apparent as with other cars, but they still exist. One example is the case of the Santa Fe's *Tulsan* streamliner, which in the early 1950s carried chair cars and a parlor observation between its namesake and Kansas City, where it made connections to Chicago.

At Kansas City Union Station, the *Tulsan's* parlor observation and last chair car were switched onto the rear end of another Santa Fe streamliner, the *Chicagoan*. The *Chicagoan* originated in Dallas without an observation car, but it left Kansas City for Chicago carrying the obs car it got from the *Tulsan*.

On the westward trip, these connections were reversed. The *Kansas Cityan* brought the parlor-obs and chair car from Chicago to Kansas City, where they were switched from the rear of the Dallas-bound train (the *Kansas Cityan*) and coupled onto the rear of the westbound *Tulsan*.

This Chicago & North Western local shows how a passenger consist could look when it wasn't turned at one end of its route. With baggage-express and baggage-RPO cars on the rear, train 706 is at Rockford, Ill., on August 16, 1947. *Elliot Kahn photo*

In a case of an exception proving the rule, here's the Baltimore & Ohio's *Ambassador* running with two sleepers right behind the tender of its P-7 Pacific. Then come two coaches and a combine on the rear end. At the time of this November 1953 photo, the train arrived at Washington, D.C., from Detroit behind diesel power. The section continuing to Baltimore was pulled backward out of Washington Union Terminal and proceeded as seen here at Relay, Md., with a 4-6-2 hauling its reversed consist. *Elliot Kahn photo*

► When the Union Pacific reinstated its *Challenger* economy trains as a *Streamliner* service in 1954, the consist looked like this view of eastbound train 108. There are two sleepers on the rear end, and then a café-lounge car that served first-class passengers only. Ahead of the café-lounge are five chair cars, and ahead of them a diner and lounge car for the coach passengers. A baggage-express car is tucked in behind three E units as the train crosses Cajon Creek at Devore, Calif., exercising UP trackage rights over the Santa Fe. *William D. Middleton photo*

Dome cars

There are no specific placements typical for dome cars. Their place in a train is determined by the basic car type beneath the dome. A dome coach goes with the coaches; a dome sleeper goes with the other sleepers. A dome lounge may go next to the diner, and a dome diner might be between the coaches and sleepers. A dome observation car would ride at the rear end of the train.

Typical consists

With these general guidelines it's possible to set up any number of logical passenger train consists. Here, for instance, is an overnight limited, our railroad's best train. We'll say the era is the early 1950s, so the equipment is all lightweight:
- Locomotive (two EMD E8 A units back-to-back)
- Baggage-mail (30-foot RPO apartment, storage mail)
- 64-seat coach (short-distance passengers)
- 48-seat chair car (through passengers)
- Dormitory-lounge car
- 36-seat dining car
- 6-section, 6-roomette, 4-bedroom sleeper
- 10-section, 6-bedroom sleeper
- 4-drawing-room, 1-bedroom lounge observation

Here's a daylight train between two large cities, again all lightweight. This train is going to handle Railway Express Agency service to intermediate stations:

Mixed-train consists

Great Northern train 61, the Minneapolis-to-Hutchinson, Minn., mixed train, has its baggage-coach combine behind the freight cars. The combine has its own heating as shown by the smoke jack on the roof, so it's equipped to run behind the freight cars and not be connected to a steam line from the locomotive. On this train the combine is also serving as the caboose. *William D. Middleton photo*

When you want to run a mixed passenger and freight train, where does the passenger car – most often a baggage-coach combine – go in the train? The general answer is that it can go at either end depending on how the car is heated. If the car has its own stove or stoves, it doesn't need to be connected to the locomotive for steam and can go on the rear end behind the freight cars. In that case it most often serves as the caboose as well.

If the combine or other passenger car depends on steam for heat, then it has to be right behind the locomotive because freight cars don't have steam lines to make a connection through the train. In that case, there typically will be a caboose at the rear of the train following the freight cars.

And though there are two ways to do this, generally any one railroad would equip its mixed train cars to operate all one way or all the other. Climate might be a factor, with lines in colder territories preferring to use steam heat.

Even if your railroad is freelanced, it probably would be a good idea to follow the practice of a prototype in the same general area.

Modeling opportunities

Add cars to regular consists. Your road's overnight limited might need an extra sleeper on Friday and Sunday to handle the surge of weekend travelers. In holiday seasons, more baggage-express cars might be required for mail and express. When the strawberry harvest comes in, express reefers can carry the berries to big-city markets quickly at the head of your passenger trains. Establish ordinary consists to set a base level, so these occasional additions will look out of the ordinary.

Break some rules – selectively. Run a local train with the baggage car or cars on the rear in one direction only, to show that it's not worth the railroad's trouble to turn such a lowly train. Carry a chair car on the rear of a train behind the Pullmans, to call attention to that car's having been added at an intermediate station. But don't just line up cars willy-nilly – the fun is having a reason to do something out of the ordinary.

Different trains serve different purposes. Just like freight train consists, passenger consists reflect a train's mission and reason for being. Take advantage of the variety in types of cars to distinguish your road's long-haul luxury liner from its intercity day train and its all-stops accommodation. Or if your railroad is trying to keep its passenger-service expense to a minimum, pare the service back to a single train each way serving as many different purposes as possible.

Follow prototype consists. Even as a freelancer it may be to your advantage to follow the consist examples of a similar prototype road. You can base your freelance trains on the equivalent trains of a favorite prototype, or use a parallel prototype as an example of the level of service justified by that travel market. But if your freelanced line parallels a major passenger carrier, management may decide

Breaking the rules with a reason, the Delaware & Hudson has a dining car right behind the baggage car on its southbound *Laurentian* at Mechanicville, N.Y., in 1968. This is a day train from Montreal to New York City, but the D&H Alco diesels, baggage car, and diner will terminate at Albany. There the three cars on the rear – two chair cars and an ex-New York Central sleeper used as a parlor car – will be uncoupled to continue south on the Penn Central's former NYC Hudson River line. *William D. Middleton photo*

it's not worth trying to compete and schedule a minimal, if respectable, service.

Use consists to reflect prosperity or hard times. In the leanest years of the Great Depression, passenger trains shrank in proportion to falling ticket sales. The same trend was obvious as passengers deserted trains for highways and airlines in the 1960s. When economic conditions improved in the late 1930s, railroads scrambled to add cars to their popular new streamliners and economy trains. After the Second World War, the trend was to launch new streamliners and re-equip existing passenger trains to take advantage of the expected peacetime boom. When you want your model railroad to reflect a particular time, your passenger train consists can make a significant contribution to the overall picture.

- Locomotive (4-6-4)
- Baggage-express (express messenger)
- Baggage-bar-lounge (smoker)
- 48-seat chair car
- 48-seat chair car
- 48-seat chair car
- lunch-counter-lounge car
- parlor car

Here's an all-stops local train with heavyweight equipment:
- Locomotive (EMD GP7 with steam generator)
- Baggage-express (express messenger)
- Baggage-mail (30-foot RPO, express)
- 72-seat coach (smoker)
- 72-seat coach

And here's a push-pull commuter train into the big city (the cab car leads on the inbound trip, and the locomotive leads outbound):
- Gallery coach/cab car
- Gallery coach
- Gallery coach
- Gallery coach
- Gallery coach
- Locomotive (EMD GP7 with HEP generator)

Prototype consists

FOUR

Bob Chapman built this HO model of the Baltimore & Ohio's *National Limited* streamliner by kitbashing Rivarossi and Bachmann cars to represent the B&O's modernized heavyweights. Since his aim was to duplicate the prototype consist, he knew exactly which cars to model and how to arrange them in the train. He described the project in the March and April 2002 issues of *Model Railroader* magazine. Model Railroader *photo by Bill Zuback*

When you can find consists for prototype trains you want to model, you don't have to guess. You can arrange your cars in the same order as the actual train and enjoy running a realistic replica of that prototype. Because they operated as scheduled services with specific equipment, we can model the consists of passenger trains with much greater accuracy than we can usually manage for freight trains. And the setouts, pickups, and connections indicated in prototype consists show how en route switching allowed some passenger and mail trains to serve cities and towns far beyond their core routes.

I've gathered some examples of prototype consists so you can see how trains are typically put together. Some of them, at least, demonstrate the guidelines for assembling consists suggested in Chapter Three.

Espee's *Coaster*

The first example (on page 62) is a secondary overnight train from the late 1940s, the Southern Pacific's *Coaster* between San Francisco and Los Angeles via its Coast Line route. First note that it follows the classic formation of head-end cars, coaches, diner, sleepers, and observation.

The source listed on page 62 specifies that even though the all-heavyweight consist was mostly the railroad's standard Dark Olive, and Pullman Green on the sleepers, a couple head-end cars were carrying the colors of SP streamliners. The SP was notable for having three different streamliner paint schemes in service by 1946, including *City Streamliner* yellow and gray, *Daylight* red and orange, and *Cascade/Lark* two-tone gray (similar to Pullman's two-tone gray). Espee would soon add two variations on red and silver with its *Golden State* and *Sunset Limited* streamliners. Even at this fairly early date the streamliner colors were appearing on heavyweight cars and spilling over onto unstreamlined services.

The *Coaster's* tourist Pullmans represent a form of economy service begun in the Great Depression year 1934. Using older cars with all-section floor plans – in some cases converted from other configurations – budget-conscious travelers were offered sleeping accommodations at rates in between standard Pullman service and coach travel.

By the late 1940s, however, the public saw both heavyweight cars and open sections as outdated, and tourist Pullman service after World War II was short-lived.

Modeling opportunities

Concentrate on featured cars to economize your modeling time (and budget). If every car of a favorite consist isn't available off the shelf, put your efforts into modeling the distinctive or featured cars that define the train's identity. (Or look for brass models of those cars if they've ever been made.) You can fill out the train with more generic stand-in models and still put together a recognizable consist.

Cut duplicate cars for layout-size consists. When the prototype train you want to model is so long that it would overpower your layout, omit some or all duplicates of basic baggage cars, coaches, and sleeping cars. Keep the train's featured cars, such as lounges, observations, diners, and domes, as they help to establish its distinctive identity.

Look for modeling and operating interest in secondary trains. Your favorite railroad's flagship streamliner gets most of the publicity, but there may be more modeling fun in an accommodation or mail train. Mixtures of heavyweight and lightweight equipment, cars to and from connecting railroads, and online passenger-train switching may all be easier to find a step or two down the timetable.

Think about modeling the Sixties. The 1960s were a decade of decline in rail passenger travel, but that doesn't mean they weren't interesting times for passenger train modelers. In some

Budd tavern-lounge-observations acquired secondhand from the New York Central were the most distinctive cars on Kansas City Southern trains 9 and 10. When Andy modeled one of these four-car New Orleans-Shreveport streamliners for a *Model Railroader* article, he thought a reasonably prototypical observation car was the most important part of the project. That made it worthwhile to kitbash the HO scale car shown above from a Con-Cor Budd dome-observation, but today he'd only have to add KCS lettering to the Walthers NYC tavern-lounge-observation shown in Chapter Two. *Model Railroader* photo by A.L. Schmidt

cases, consists shrank to more easily modeled "pike-size" proportions. As railroads consolidated their services into fewer trains, the remaining trains often did more extensive switching en route to maintain connections. Passenger-train consists sometimes included container or piggyback cars for more efficient handling of mail and express or just to earn some additional

continued on page 54

The open-platform Pullman observation car on this train enjoyed a brief revival after being discontinued during WWII, when most such equipment was sidetracked in favor of cars with greater passenger capacity. Nevertheless, the sleeper observation would soon be replaced by one of the railroad's own heavyweight smoker-lounge-observations, and then in the spring of 1947, all open-platform observations would be withdrawn from service on SP trains. Whatever nostalgic value they hold for us today, they were seen as obsolete in railroading's streamliner age.

Great Northern's Empire Builder

This consist (on page 63) represents one of the first long-distance streamliners to enter service in the postwar period. It took until the beginning of 1947 for enough lightweight streamlined cars to be produced for the five 12-car train sets needed to support a Chicago-Seattle service.

Again this train demonstrates the classic formation from front to rear. There's only a single head-end car, but it includes a 30-foot Railway Post Office apartment for mail service. It also carries water tanks in its baggage section to supply extra water for the locomotives' steam generators, a precaution against the bitter winters of the Great Northern's route through the Northwest.

Although coach passengers could use the dining car if they wished, the *Lake*-series coffee-shop car offered cheaper meal service for those traveling on a budget. The *Lake* car also incorporated a 10-seat lounge area for coach passengers and dormitory space for the dining car and coffee-shop crews.

The 16-4 *Glacier*-series sleepers made use of duplex roomettes at staggered heights. These offered the privacy passengers increasingly sought while increasing the capacity of both single cars and the train. Sections were still provided in the 8-4-4 *Pass* cars, and for many years these were the most costly accommodations allowed for passengers traveling on government expense accounts.

While it presented a uniformly colorful appearance in striking Omaha Orange and Pullman Green, the *Builder* was actually a pool train operated jointly with two other railroads. The Chicago, Burlington & Quincy provided the connection between the Windy

continued from page 53

revenue from high-priority freight. Locomotive consists as well were more varied and less stereotyped than in the streamliners' heyday, with more trains powered by road switchers or by coupled road switchers and cab units.

Use prototypical power by motorizing a head-end car. Sometimes the scale version of the locomotive that powered a real passenger train has a hard time handling a full-length model consist, especially one made up of heavy brass equipment. A motorized power truck concealed in a baggage car or combine can act as an unseen helper for that underpowered Pacific or 4-4-2. If you use Digital Command Control, you can equalize the speed curves of the two "units" so they'll run together smoothly.

Top left: One challenge in modeling a train like this Southern Pacific heavyweight *Sunset Limited* is that a model of its medium-size P-6 class Pacific may not have enough pulling power for the train's 12-car consist. *Harold K. Vollrath collection*

Left: Here's a way to handle prototype-length consists with underpowered locomotives. These self-contained HO power trucks imported by The Coach Yard are designed to be concealed in a baggage car or the baggage end of a combine. Like unseen helpers, they can add their power to that of the road engine. *Model Railroader photo*

Complete trains

A few famous trains are offered by passenger car manufacturers either in boxed sets or in series of individual cars. The photos here show the original 1949 *California Zephyr* from an N scale set by Kato. The set makes up a complete 11-car consist. Since this train was jointly operated by three railroads as described in Chapter One, Kato is also separately offering suitable Chicago, Burlington & Quincy; Denver & Rio Grande Western; and Western Pacific diesel locomotives.

The *California Zephyr's* cars all carried the train name on their main letter boards, with the initials of the railroad owning each car on small letter boards at each end. It followed the style of the Burlington's *Zephyrs* in giving each car in the consist a name beginning with the word "Silver."

From front to rear, the Budd-built *California Zephyr* begins with a 70-foot baggage-express car, the CB&Q *Silver Bear*, and a dome coach seating 46 passengers, the D&RGW *Silver Bronco*. The dome space was unreserved and not counted in the car's seating capacity. *Andy Sperandeo photos*

The third and fourth cars are dome coaches seating 46 passengers each, the CB&Q *Silver Ranch* and the WP *Silver Feather*. The latter name was a reminder that the Western Pacific advertised itself as the Feather River Route, after its scenic, low-grade route through California's Sierra Nevada.

The CB&Q *Silver Club* was a dome-dormitory-buffet-lounge car. It included sleeping space for the train's onboard service crew and served light meals and beverages to coach passengers. Next up was the first of the train's five sleepers, an example of the popular 10-roomette, 6-double-bedroom type of car. This is the Burlington's *Silver Valley*.

The D&RGW *Silver Glacier* was another 10-6 sleeper. The *California Zephyr* 10-6s were unusual in having a separate window opposite each bedroom on the aisle side of the car – the six windows to the right on this car. *Silver Diner* was a CB&Q 40-seat dining car featuring four booths seating four each as well as eight four-seat tables.

Lightweight all-section sleeping cars were unusual, especially in the postwar era, but there was one 16-section sleeper like the D&RGW *Silver Aspen* in each original *California Zephyr* consist. As the salability of section space declined, these cars were rebuilt as coaches in the 1960s. The WP *Silver Canyon* is a third 10-6 sleeping car.

The *California Zephyr* observation cars were distinctive sleeper-lounge-dome-observations like the D&RGW *Silver Sky*. The sleeping accommodations were three double bedrooms and one drawing room that included the luxury of a shower. The roof behind the dome was higher than in front for headroom in the raised observation lounge.

City and the beginning of GN rails in St. Paul, Minn. On the "Q" the train was pulled by diesels sheathed in stainless steel and sporting the 9900-series numbers of the Burlington's *Zephyrs*.

In fact, the Burlington was such a partner in the *Builder's* operation that it owned 12 of the original cars, equivalent to one complete train. Though painted in GN colors, the Q cars carried the initials "CB&Q" at the ends of their letter boards, where the *Builder's* other cars were lettered "Great Northern."

Toward the western end of its run, the *Empire Builder* set off a 48-seat coach and an 8-4-4 sleeper at Spokane, Wash., to continue to Portland, Ore., by way of the Spokane, Portland & Seattle. The eastbound *Builder* picked up the two cars from Portland and so provided through service from Chicago to the two largest cities of the Pacific Northwest. This is a good example of how even a railroad's flagship trains can be involved in en route switching.

B&O mail train

Baltimore & Ohio No. 29 (page 64) was both ordinary and remarkable. It was ordinary because there were once many such trains across the country dedicated to handling mail and express traffic. It was remarkable because of the many connections it made between cities both along and beyond its route. Almost anything that a mail train might be called upon to do, No. 29 did.

It set out four cars at various points for connections with other B&O trains and received two cars at Parkersburg from B&O No. 23. It delivered seven cars to connections with other railroads. Two cars from Philadelphia continued on other lines all the way to the West Coast.

Unlike the B&O's passenger-carrying trains, mail train 29 didn't take the time to call at Washington Union Station. Its cars to and from WUS were handled by a switch engine meeting No. 29 at the outlying QN Tower.

On No. 29's overnight trek from Jersey City to Cincinnati, an old heavyweight coach without air-conditioning served as a rider car for the train crew and deadheading railroaders. West of Cincinnati, however, the daytime local passenger business was sufficient to warrant a newer air-conditioned lightweight coach.

Number 29 carried mail in sealed storage cars, working storage and baggage cars, and Railway Post Office cars. It carried both sealed and working express

8 pike-size passenger trains

Short trains you can model realistically in HO and N scales

cars. And it carried as many as twice the usual number of cars in a long passenger train. It demonstrates plenty of opportunities for a freelance mail train of similar size and range.

MoPac's *Texas Eagle*

As ridership declined in the late 1950s and early 1960s, railroads sought to control their costs both by eliminating trains and by having their remaining trains serve multiple purposes. By 1965, the Missouri Pacific's *Texas Eagle* (page 65) was an example of how wide-ranging a passenger operation could be even in what were definitely its waning years.

As the consist list for MoPac No. 1 demonstrates, the railroad was attempting to maintain a decent level of service and connections by handling as much of the remaining business as it could with one big train. The *Texas Eagle* of that summer rivaled the B&O mail train in the variety of connections it made and destinations it served. It carried through cars for places as diverse as Alexandria, La.; Harlingen, Texas; Los Angeles; and even Mexico City. Its switching in the passenger stations at Little Rock, Texarkana, and Longview would offer plenty of challenge for model railroad station crews. (Note the baggage cars on the rear of the train leaving Little Rock for easier setout at subsequent stops.)

The consist indicates too that the *Texas Eagle* wasn't just one train but a network.

Besides No. 1 between St. Louis and San Antonio, there were No. 21 between New Orleans and Fort Worth and No. 41 between Palestine and Houston. Four of No. 1's St. Louis cars continued from San Antonio to Laredo as part of the *Aztec Eagle*, also scheduled as train No. 1. There were lesser connections without the *Eagle* cachet.

The *Texas Eagle* not only offered coaches, sleepers, and meal service on all its routes (with dome coaches on trains 1 and 21), it was the MoPac's primary mail and express carrier on these lines. Although the MoP of the mid-1960s had sharply reduced its passenger-train miles compared to the previous decade, it was still serving a broad market.

Amtrak's *Eagle*

When Amtrak began operating a pared-down national rail passenger network in 1971, it at first maintained exisiting services on a few select routes. As it acquired new locomotives and cars to replace the hand-me-downs

This is an N scale model of the Santa Fe's Amarillo-Lubbock trains, nos. 93 and 94, assembled with Kato models. With one diesel and three cars, it's within our definition of a pike-size passenger train. Jim Forbes photo

A small model railroad doesn't have to limit your ambition to run trains of realistic length, especially in passenger service. All you have to do is model a pike-size passenger train, a prototype consist with five or fewer cars pulled by a single steam locomotive or at most two diesel units.

The idea, introduced to *Model Railroader* readers by author Mike Schafer back in 1980, is to find real trains that can be represented in their entirety without overwhelming average-size layouts.

We asked the *Model Railroader* staff to select a train and briefly describe how it could be modeled. And instead of listing only HO scale models, we're offering some N scale consists too.

All eight trains here can be replicated with either ready-to-run or kit models. Some of these cars and locomotives may be a little harder to find than others, but we think a reasonably determined model railroader has a fighting chance of assembling any of these trains, without spending the next couple of mortgage payments!

When no model is available that's an exact match, we've called for stand-in cars or locomotives. These are at least similar to the prototypes. Anyone looking for a greater modeling challenge is welcome to go beyond our choices to build or buy more-accurate cars and engines.

A lot of the fun of passenger-train modeling is that we can learn with some precision which cars and locomotives operated on specific trains. We can then assemble consists that aren't just collections of "typical" equipment but scale models of real trains. And if we pick our prototypes carefully, they'll still fit on most of our layouts.

continued on page 58

inherited from traditional railroads, it was able to re-establish service on some routes it had initially omitted. The consists of the Amtrak *Eagle* of the early 1980s (page 66) represent such a train. It offered daily service between Chicago and St. Louis and four-days-a-week service between St. Louis and San Antonio.

Amtrak's *Eagle* service was obviously much simpler and used many fewer cars than the old *Texas Eagle*. The trains nevertheless offered all the essentials of MoPac rail passenger travel, including sleeping accommodations on the overnight journey to and from Texas.

Baggage and express space was provided without head-end cars by taking advantage of the double-deck configuration of the Superliner equipment. Note that unlike the old single-level baggage-coach combines, Superliner baggage-coaches can be placed anywhere in a train without restricting passengers from passing through the car.

Amtrak's *Southwest Chief*

Train No. 3 as observed at Los Angeles on June 28, 2005, is a good example of today's long-distance Amtrak service (page 67). Indeed, instead of being immediately turned back at Chicago, after servicing and cleaning the eastbound consist usually continues on to Washington, D.C., as another train. This formation can thus also be taken as representative of Amtrak's *James Whitcomb Riley*. The train has sleeping cars on both ends, but as the Superliner portion of the consist isn't always turned at terminals, this isn't as significant as it was earlier.

From the 1990s into the first years of the new century, Amtrak was actively competing for mail and express traffic. In those years the *Southwest Chief* usually carried material-handling cars (MHCs), express boxcars, express mechanical refrigerator cars, and even RoadRailer intermodal vans in addition to a traditional baggage car or two from Amtrak's Heritage Fleet. The MHC's were equipped with HEP (head-end-power) cables and, like the baggage cars, could run between the locomotives and the passenger cars. As the express boxcars lacked HEP equipment, they had to trail behind the passenger-carrying cars. Conventional equipment could not be coupled behind RoadRailers, so they brought up the rear of the train.

Although the passenger equipment wasn't switched en route, the express cars and vans often were. Between Kansas City and

---

continued from page 57

Fred M. Springer photo

Atchison, Topeka & Santa Fe trains 93 and 94
The *West Texas Express* (93), and *Eastern Express* (94), Amarillo-Lubbock, Texas, 1955-65

Santa Fe's streamliners mostly exceeded our pike-size parameters, but trains on AT&SF feeder lines offer short-consist modeling opportunities. Trains 93 and 94 connected with the popular *San Francisco Chief* at Amarillo to offer through sleeping car and connecting chair car service between Chicago and Lubbock. Locomotive 80L, an E8m rebuilt by Electro-Motive Division from one of the Santa Fe's earliest E1 passenger diesels, was the regular power after these locomotive-hauled trains replaced a gas-electric motor car ("doodlebug") on this run in 1955.

These trains can be modeled in either N or HO scale pretty much just by opening boxes. In N, the Kato Budd 10-roomette, 6-bedroom sleeper can be used as a stand-in for the fluted-side Pullman-Standard 10-roomette, 3-bedroom, 2-compartment sleeper of the *Blue* series that operated on this line in the trains' earliest years. Or use the Kato smooth-side Pullman 6-section, 6-roomette, 4-bedroom *Valley*-series car, as this type of car replaced the *Blues* in 1957. In HO, you can use the Walthers 6-6-4 Pullman-Standard sleeper to model the trains with *Valley*-series equipment, or you can build a *Blue*-series car using etched and plated car sides sold by the Santa Fe Ry. Historical & Modeling Society. These may be used with core body kits made by Eastern Car Works or Train Station Products. – A.S.

Santa Fe models

N scale: Kato no. 176-5304 E8 and no. 106-1604 passenger car set (baggage, chair car, and sleeper only, not using the dome car), or use a *Valley*-series smooth-side sleeper from Kato set no. 106-1401 instead of the fluted 10-6

HO scale: Life-Like no. 30793 or 94 E8 (A unit only); Walthers no. 932-6405 baggage-express, no. 932-6305 chair car, and no. 932-6722 6-6-4 sleeper

Los Angeles, the *Southwest Chief* often stretched to more than 20 cars of all types.

After 2003, Amtrak reduced its commitment to express traffic. It still handles some in its baggage cars and occasionally adds a couple of its ExpressTrak mechanical reefers to the rear of the eastbound *Southwest Chief*.

Amtrak California Pacific Surfliners

Amtrak and the state of California are partners in operating *Pacific Surfliner* service (page 67), which runs intercity trains over the former Atchison, Topeka & Santa Fe Surf Line and former Southern Pacific Coast Line routes. The *Pacific Surfliners* are powered by Electro-Motive F59PHI locomotives with 3,200 hp for traction and separate diesel-generator sets for head-end power (HEP). The trains consist of double-deck cars built by M-K Amerail in Hornell, N.Y. (Scale drawings of the locomotives and cars appeared in the November 1997 *Model Railroader*.)

The Amerail California cars are the same height as Amtrak's Superliners, 16'-1", but have two lower-level entrance doors on each side. The cars have both HEP connections and multiple-unit (m.u.) cables, so trains can operate in push-pull fashion with the locomotive controlled from a cab car on the other end.

On weekdays there are two *Pacific Surfliners* each way connecting San Luis Obispo, Los Angeles, and San Diego; three each way between Goleta (one stop north of Santa Barbara), Los Angeles, and San Diego; and seven each way between Los Angeles and San Diego (according to Amtrak schedules effective April 25, 2005). Passenger-train fans might miss stainless *San Diegans* pulled by Santa Fe warbonnet diesels and the red-and-orange *Daylights* of the SP, but those famous trains didn't offer half the trips of today's *Pacific Surfliner* service.

The consists show two representative trains. Locomotives lead southbound and coach-baggage cab cars lead northbound. The Pacific Business Class cars offer a premium, reserved-seat service, and the cafe cars offer sandwiches, snacks, and beverages on all trains.

In addition to the *Pacific Surfliners*, similar equipment operates in the *Capitol* corridor between Sacramento, Oakland, and San Jose and in the *San Joaquin* corridor between Oakland and Bakersfield.

Jim Scribbins photo

Soo Line trains 1 and 2
Chicago, Ill.-St. Paul, Minn., 1946-53

Trains 1 and 2 were typical of many short passenger trains the Minneapolis, St. Paul & Sault Ste. Marie (Soo Line) operated throughout its seven-state system. Although they carried passengers, the trains hauled more mail and express than people. A usual consist for trains 1 and 2 in the late 1940s and early '50s included a Railway Post Office-baggage-express car, a combination baggage-coach or sometimes just a baggage-express car, and an air-conditioned cafe-coach, all pulled by one of the Soo's 4-6-2 Pacifics. The trains would also carry a baggage-express car between Chicago and Waukesha, Wis.

Modeling trains 1 and 2 in HO scale will involve a few evenings' work but won't be too difficult. An Athearn Genesis United States Railroad Administration light Pacific can stand in for a Soo 4-6-2 – letter an undecorated model with Microscale decal set 87-1136. For passenger cars, Rivarossi's heavyweight RPO, baggage car, and coach would be close, and a second baggage car could be used for the Waukesha express car. Like the locomotive, the cars aren't exact matches, but Rivarossi offers the models painted in Pennsylvania RR Tuscan Red, which is a lot like Soo Line Maroon. The Soo Line Historical & Technical Society offers HO scale Soo passenger car decals for $3 a set plus $1 shipping. (To order, visit the Web site at www.sooline.org.) – *David Popp*

Soo Line models

HO scale: Athearn no. 9040 undec. 4-6-2; Rivarossi PRR no. 2806 RPO-baggage, no. 6567 baggage car (2), and no. 2738 coach (see above for decals)

continued on page 60

continued from page 59

Great Northern Ry. photo

3 Great Northern trains 11 and 12
The *Red River*, Minneapolis, Minn.-Grand Forks, N.D., 1950-68

The *Red River* wore the classic GN Omaha Orange and Pullman Green and would look great on an Upper Midwest layout. Eastbound, train 12 connected with the Chicago, Burlington & Quincy's *Afternoon Zephyr* in the Twin Cities to offer service to Chicago. The CB&Q's *Morning Zephyr* connected with train 11 for Chicago-Grand Forks service. Locomotive 512, an Electro-Motive E7, was the normally assigned power.

The *Red River* can be modeled to varying degrees of accuracy in HO and N scales. In HO, Northstar Railroad Models offers kits based on Eastern Car Works cores with laser-cut acrylic sides specifically designed for the *Red River*. The Broadway Limited E7 has even been offered as GN 512.

In N, Con-Cor's 85-foot smooth-side coaches, Railway Post Office-baggage car, and observation car can serve as stand-ins for the GN's equipment. Use an undecorated Con-Cor E7, and give it GN paint and Microscale decals from set no. 60-45.
– *Cody Grivno*

GN models

HO scale: Broadway Limited no. 608 E7A; Northstar Railroad Models no. 1100 RPO-baggage car, two no. 2100 60-seat coaches, no. 2101 conductor's coach, and no. 6100 observation cafe-parlor car

N scale: Con-Cor no. 1-0028203 E7, no. 140214 RPO-baggage car, three no. 140014 coaches, and no. 140414 observation car

Elmer Treolar photo

4 New York Central trains 333 and 334
Bay City-Detroit, Mich., 1949

Most passenger traffic on the Water Level Route was east-west, but a few trains ran north-south, including this one, which carried vacationers north from Detroit (where they connected with no. 44). Never as long as the east-west trains, 333 and 334 offer ideal pike-size consists. In this photo taken June 3, 1949, no. 334 had J-1 Hudson no. 5340, a baggage-express car, a Railway Post Office-baggage combine, a baggage-coach combine, a heavyweight coach, and a New York-Bay City 10-roomette, 6-double-bedroom Pullman.

In either N or HO, start with the Hudson of your choice and end with a Rivarossi 10-6 smooth-side sleeper. (Through the end of May 1949, the train carried an 8-section, 1-drawing room, 2-compartment heavyweight sleeper.)

It's in between that things get tricky. In HO, a Rivarossi baggage car would be a good stand-in, as would a Rivarossi baggage-RPO. In each case, replacing the trucks with four-wheel versions would go a long way toward obtaining the New York Central look. For the HO coach, you could build the Funaro & Camarlengo no. 5070 resin kit, assemble the Branchline Trains NYC coach, or use a Bachmann P70 coach (no. 89405) as a stand-in. Likewise, the Bachmann combine is the closest match in HO at this time.

In N, however, once you get past the sleeper, you'd need to use Rivarossi or Model Power (Lima) cars as stand-ins, and even those won't be terribly close. You could kitbash one end of a baggage car onto a coach to make the combine, but the windows would still be in pairs, PRR-style. – *Terry Thompson*

NYC models

HO scale: Broadway Limited no. 3 Hudson; Rivarossi no. 6561 baggage, no. 2395 RPO, and no. 2709 Pullman; Bachmann no. 89405 or Funaro & Camarlengo no. 5070 coach; Bachmann combine

N scale: Con-Cor no. 1003006 Hudson; Rivarossi or Model Power standard baggage, coach, and combine; Rivarossi streamlined sleeper

Phillip R. Hastings photo

5 Chicago & North Western *Kate Shelley 400* trains 1 and 2   Chicago, Ill.-Boone, Iowa, 1967-71

The train pictured was still known locally as the *Kate*, but officially, at this point in 1971, it was simply designated train 1 (or 2). The *Kate Shelley 400*, named for a 15-year-old Iowa farm girl who heroically saved the lives of two railroad employees following a bridge collapse, was announced in 1947 with grand intentions. When she actually began running in 1955, the *Kate* was a somewhat stripped-down version and declined through more-utilitarian consists to a single Electro-Motive E7 and a pair of 800-series lightweight coaches by June of 1967.

Trains 1 and 2 can be credibly modeled in both N and HO. In N, Con-Cor has offered E7s in a variety of schemes and undecorated. Con-Cor sells 85-foot smooth-side coaches in C&NW yellow and green. If you're not content with "close enough," Brass Car Sides offers 56-seat 400 coach sides, no. 173-501. Microscale Decals has C&NW sets, no. 60-51 for the locomotive and 60-859 for the coaches.

In HO scale, the Broadway Limited E7 in C&NW paint will do nicely, and you can use Rivarossi's coaches in North Western colors. Brass Car Sides offers 56-seat North Western coach sides, no. 173-1, so you can make your own if you prefer. Locomotive and passenger car decals are again available from Microscale, nos. 87-51 and 87-859.
– *Dick Christianson*

North Western models

HO scale: Broadway Limited no. 617 or 618 E7A; two Rivarossi no. 635-6715 coaches

N scale: Con-Cor no. 1-0028203 E7A, two no. 1-04001T coaches

Jim Hediger photo

6 Amtrak-Via trains 364 and 365 the *International* (366 and 367 on Sundays) Chicago, Ill.-Toronto, Ont., Canada, present day

The *International* runs over both Amtrak's own rails and the Grand Trunk Western between Chicago and Port Huron, Mich., it crosses the border through Canadian National's tunnel under the St. Clair River, and it uses CN track between Sarnia and Toronto. The normal consist includes coaches and a combined food-service and custom-class car (missing from the train on the day I photographed it). The F40PH locomotive is supplied alternately by Amtrak or Via.

The Phase III train can be modeled in HO using a Walthers' Amtrak or Via F40PH and Amtrak Horizon Fleet coaches. However, since its inception in the 1980s the *International* has used Amtrak Heritage, Amfleet I and II, and Horizon cars in almost any combination. Walthers offers all these car styles, and Con-Cor makes Heritage cars.

A similar N scale consist can be made with a Life-Like Amtrak F40PH and three Bachmann Amfleet coaches. Substitute Con-Cor Budd Heritage cars if you prefer. – *Jim Hediger*

International models

HO scale: Walthers no. 931-308 Via F40PH, no. 932-6051 Horizon coach, and no. 932-6061 Horizon food service car

N scale: Life-Like no. 933-7641 Amtrak F40PH and Bachmann no. 160-72255 Amfleet coaches, or Con-Cor no. 223-420109 Budd Heritage coaches

continued on page 62

Consist Table 1
Southern Pacific *Coaster*

Nearing the end of its overnight run from Los Angeles, the Southern Pacific's train 69, the *Coaster*, greets the morning sun at Bayshore, Calif., south of San Francisco. On this late-1940s day, a streamlined GS-4-class 4-8-4 is in charge of the all-heavyweight consist. The *Coaster* was the secondary accommodation train on the same route as the all-Pullman *Lark*. D.K. Hedgpeth photo

Overnight accomodation train between Los Angeles and San Francisco, all heavyweight, cars painted Dark Olive (SP) or Pullman Green (Pullman) except as noted. Typical fall 1946 consist for westbound – toward San Francisco – train No. 69 (from *Southern Pacific Passenger Trains, Vol. 1 – Night Trains of the Coast Line*, by Ryan and Shine).

- Locomotive, MT-1 class 4-8-2 Mountain
- Baggage-express, class 70-B-8, operating as mail storage car daily except Sunday (*Lark* two-tone gray)
- Baggage-express, class 60-B-6
- Baggage-express, class 70-B-9 (*Daylight* red and orange)
- Coach, class 60-C-4, 72 seats
- Coach, class 60-C-4, 54 seats, news agent
- Coach, class 60-C-5, 72 seats
- Coach, class 60-C-4, 72 seats
- Diner, class 77-D-9, 36 seats
- 16-section tourist sleeper*, Pullman 4100 series
- 16-section tourist sleeper, Pullman 4100 series
- 16-section tourist sleeper, Pullman 4100 series
- 10-1-2** sleeper, Pullman *Camp* series
- 10-section-lounge-observation***, Pullman *Mount* series

(On Friday and Sunday two more coaches were added behind the last baggage-express cars, making the train length 13 cars Monday-Thursday and Saturday, 15 cars Friday, and 14 cars on Sunday.)

* Tourist Pullmans were older sleepers with 16 or 14 sections offering lower fares than standard Pullman rates.
** 10-1-2: 10 sections, 1 drawing room, 2 compartments.
*** Replaced by SP smoker-lounge-observation, class 77-O-1, in early 1947, but in spring 1947 all open-platform observations were withdrawn from service on SP trains.

---

continued from page 61

J. David Ingles photo

7 Conrail trains 453-343 and 455-456
Chicago, Ill.-Valparaiso, Ind., 1979

A Conrail passenger train? West of New Jersey? Yes, and it has two types of power and three types of coaches. The "Valpo" locals were the last vestiges of the Pennsylvania RR's Chicago commuter service, and they hung on through the Penn Central years and into Conrail (and eventually Amtrak) before being discontinued in 1991. Pennsy P70 coaches (with both round and clerestory roofs) and steam-generator-equipped Geeps were typical fare in the 1970s. Other equipment also showed up, including E8s, former Erie-Lackawanna smooth-side coaches, and former New York Central fluted-side Pullman-Standard (P-S) coaches – in this case an Amtrak car, although Penn Central had some too.

You can model this train fairly easily if you don't mind a little painting. Conrail Geeps are easy to find in both HO and N, as are E8s, though no one offers CR black on an E8. Bachmann and Eastern Car Works offer P70 coaches in HO, and Model Power (Lima) and Rivarossi have them in N. If you bought two, you could paint one PRR Tuscan red and one PC green, and letter both for PC. The Erie-Lackawanna coach in this train is one of only 25 lightweight coaches (some American Car & Foundry, others from Pullman-Standard) the line had. A Rivarossi coach (in HO) or a Con-Cor coach (in N) can serve as stand-ins.

If you want to model the ex-NYC coach, you'd have a challenge in HO, because no manufacturer offers a Central P-S coach with fluted sides. The simplest solution would be to use either a Budd coach or a smooth-side P-S coach (many Central P-S cars had their fluting removed) as a stand-in. In N scale, look for a Rivarossi or Con-Cor fluted-side P-S coach, which is reasonably close. – *T.T.*

Conrail models

HO scale: Life-Like Proto 2000 no. 30806 E8; Atlas GP9; Bachmann no. 89245 coach; Rivarossi no. 6599 undecorated smooth-side coach; Walthers no. 6301 Amtrak coach

N scale: Kato no. 176290 E8; Atlas GP9; Model Power no. 8615 undec. heavyweight coach; Con-Cor no. 400111 E-L coach and no. 420100 undec. coach (paint Amtrak Phase I)

Consist Table 2
Great Northern Empire Builder

Brand new in 1947, the Great Northern's streamlined Empire Builder posed at St. Paul, Minn. The GN's Chicago-Seattle flagship had just been re-equipped with Pullman-standard lightweight cars. GN Ry. photo

A 1947 long-distance streamliner between Chicago and Seattle, Chicago-St. Paul via Chicago, Burlington & Quincy, all Pullman-Standard lightweight equipment (from December 1991 *Model Railroader*).

- Locomotives, E7 A-A, E5 A-B on CB&Q; GN electric locomotives pulled diesels and train between Wenatchee and Skykomish, Wash., over the Cascade Mountains and through the eight-mile Cascade Tunnel
- Mail-baggage, 1100 series   Chicago-Seattle
  (with 30-foot RPO and baggage-section water tanks for locomotive steam generators)
- 60-seat coach, 1110 series (short-distance riders)   Chicago-Seattle
- 48-seat "Day-Nite" coach, 1120 series   Chicago-Portland, Ore.
  (via Spokane, Portland & Seattle between Spokane and Portland)
- 48-seat Day-Nite coach, 1120 series   Chicago-Seattle
- 48-seat Day-Nite coach, 1120 series   Chicago-Seattle
- Coffee-shop-lounge-dormitory, *Lake*-suffix names   Chicago-Seattle
- 36-seat diner, *Lake*-prefix names   Chicago-Seattle
- 8-4-4* sleeper, *Pass*-series names   Chicago-Portland, Ore.
  (via SP&S between Spokane and Portland)
- 16-4** sleeper, *Glacier*-series names   Chicago-Seattle
- 16-4 sleeper, *Glacier* series   Chicago-Seattle
- 8-4-4 sleeper, *Pass* series   Chicago-Seattle
- 2-1*** sleeper-buffet-lounge-observation, *River*-series names   Chicago-Seattle

(12 cars Chicago-Spokane, 10 cars Spokane-Seattle.)

* 8-4-4: 8 duplex roomettes, 4 sections, 4 bedrooms.
** 16-4: 16 duplex roomettes, 4 bedrooms.
*** 2-1: 2 bedrooms, 1 drawing room.

Ben Bachmann photo

Amtrak trains 27 and 28, the Empire Builder
The Portland section, Spokane, Wash.-Portland, Ore., 1981-present

With a typical consist of coach, coach/baggage, lounge/cafe, sleeper, and material-handling car (MHC), the Portland section of Amtrak's *Empire Builder* is one of the shortest Superliner-equipped trains. Between Chicago and Spokane, the cars of the Portland section run as part of the Seattle-bound *Empire Builder*. From Spokane, a single locomotive (Electro-Motive F40PHs until the mid-1990s, then General Electric P40s and P42s) takes the little train 381 miles to Portland.

Excellent models of the train's Superliner cars, locomotives, and MHCs have been produced in HO and N scales in a variety of Amtrak stripe patterns (Phase II, as built in the early 1970s; Phase III, used in the 1980s; Phase IV, mid-1990s). In HO, alternatives include the Bachmann Spectrum F40PH or Athearn P40; Con-Cor MHC, coach, coach-baggage, sleeper, and lounge-cafe. Alternatives in N scale include the Kato General Electric P42, MHC, and four-car Superliner set. *– Carl Swanson*

Amtrak models

HO scale: Walthers Trainline no. 931-311 F40PH; Walthers no. 932-6191 lounge-cafe, no. 932-6151 coach-baggage, no. 932-6162 coach, no. 932-6171 sleeper, and no. 932-6023 MHC

N scale: Life-Like no. 433-7641 F40PH; Con-Cor no. 4642 lounge/cafe car, no. 4622 coach/baggage car, no. 4602 coach, no. 4632 sleeper, and no. 4681 MHC

Consist Table 3
Baltimore & Ohio No. 29

Lacking a photo of Baltimore & Ohio train 29, let this represent the image of a double-headed mail and express train on the B&O. We see train 23 at Tunnelton, W.Va., behind 2-8-2 Mikado no. 4633 and 4-6-2 Pacific no. 5083, on June 11, 1949. In fact, train 23 was part of train 29's complex network of connections, with train 23 handing off Washington, D.C.-to-Cincinnati storage mail and Railway Post Office cars to train 29 at Parkersburg, W.Va. *Walter H. Thrall Jr. photo*

Mail and express train between Jersey City and St. Louis, all heavyweight (October 1, 1950, consist from *Baltimore & Ohio passenger service, 1945-1971, Volume 1, The Route of the National Limited*, by Harry Stegmaier Jr. Not all car lines operated daily).

(Up to 18 cars Jersey City-Philadelphia, 26 cars Philadelphia-Baltimore, 25 cars Baltimore-Washington, 20 cars Washington-Cumberland, 18 cars Cumberland-Grafton, 15 cars Grafton-Parkersburg, 17 cars Parkersburg-Cincinnati, and 16 cars Cincinnati-St. Louis.)

* Sealed: car loaded at one point and dispatched locked to its destination.
** Working: Car has a baggage man or express messenger receiving and dispatching mail and express at stops en route.

- Locomotives, two class T-3 4-8-2 Mountains double-headed
- Baggage (storage mail)   Washington-Grafton, W.Va.
- Express (sealed*)   Washington-St. Louis
- Storage mail (sealed)   Jersey City-Baltimore
- Express (sealed)   Jersey City-Baltimore
- Express (sealed)   Jersey City-Baltimore
- Express   Philadelphia-Baltimore
- Express (sealed)   Philadelphia-Detroit
   (Set out at Philadelphia to continue on B&O No. 19 to Detroit.)
- Express (sealed)   Jersey City-Washington
- Express (sealed)   Jersey City-Washington
- Baggage-express (working**)   Jersey City-Washington
- Express (sealed)   Philadelphia-Washington
- Express (sealed)   Baltimore-Washington
- Express (sealed)   Baltimore-Jacksonville
   (Set out at Washington to continue via Richmond, Fredericksburg & Potomac and Atlantic Coast Line)
- Express (sealed)   Jersey City-Richmond
   (Set out at Washington to continue via RF&P)
- Express (newspapers)   Jersey City-Birmingham
   (Set out at Washington to continue via Southern Ry.)
- Express (newspapers)   Jersey City-Wheeling, W.Va.
   (Set out at Grafton to continue on B&O No. 343 to Wheeling)
- Express (newspapers)   Philadelphia-Clarksburg, W.Va.
   (Set out at Grafton to continue on B&O No. 11 to Clarksburg)
- Storage mail (working)   Parkersburg, W.Va.-Cincinnati
- Railway Post Office   Parkersburg, W.Va.-Cincinnati
   (Cincinnati storage mail and RPO from Washington on B&O No. 23, added to no. 29 at Parkersburg)
- Express (sealed)   Philadelphia-Cincinnati
- Baggage-express (sealed)   Jersey City-Cincinnati
- Baggage-express (working)   Jersey City-Cincinnati
- Baggage-express (sealed)   Jersey City-St. Louis
- Express (sealed)   Philadelphia-St. Louis
- Express (sealed)   Baltimore-St. Louis
- Express (sealed)   Philadelphia-Los Angeles
- Express (sealed)   Philadelphia-Oakland, Calif.
   (California cars continue to Kansas City via Missouri Pacific and to Los Angeles and Oakland via Atchison, Topeka & Santa Fe)
- Express (sealed)   Baltimore-St. Louis
- Express (sealed)   Jersey City-St. Louis
- Express (sealed)   Jersey City-St. Louis
- Express (sealed)   Jersey City-Louisville
   (Set out at Cincinnati to continue via Louisville & Nashville)
- Express (newspapers)   Jersey City-Cumberland, Md.
- Express (sealed)   Jersey City-Pittsburgh
   (Set out at Cumberland to continue on B&O No. 21 to Pittsburgh)
- Rider coach (non-air-conditioned)   Jersey City-Cincinnati
- Storage mail (sealed)   Kansas-Kansas City
   (Continues from St. Louis via Missouri Pacific)
- Storage mail (sealed)   Cincinnati-St. Louis
- Baggage (mail-working)   Cincinnati-St. Louis
- Baggage (express-working)   Cincinnati-St. Louis
- Express (sealed)   Cincinnati-St. Louis
- Air-conditioned coach   Cincinnati-St. Louis

Consist Table 4
Missouri Pacific *Texas Eagle*

The photographer has framed Missouri Pacific no. 2, the northbound *Texas Eagle*, with a baggage cart at Milano, Texas. Here the MoPac line used by the *Eagle* from San Antonio crossed the former Gulf, Colorado & Santa Fe line between Houston and Fort Worth. In this middle-1960s view, no. 2 has the mixed power consist typical of that time, an E8 and a steam-generator-equipped GP7. *Jim Hickey photo*

Train No. 1 from St. Louis to San Antonio (summer 1965 consist from *Twilight of the Great Trains*, by Fred Frailey).

- Locomotives, two or three units, almost any combination of EMD E units and GP7s with Alco PAs
- Storage mail — Texarkana-San Antonio
- Storage mail — St. Louis-San Antonio
  (St. Louis-Texarkana on MP No. 3)
- RPO-baggage — St. Louis-San Antonio
- RPO-baggage — St. Louis-Houston
- Storage mail — Texarkana-Houston
  (Previous two cars set off at Palestine, Texas, for MP *Texas Eagle* No. 41 to Houston)
- Baggage-mail-express — St. Louis-Harlingen, Texas
  (St. Louis-Texarkana on MP No. 3, set off at Palestine for MP No. 41 to Houston; MP No. 55 from Houston to Brownwood sets off this car at Harlingen)
- Storage mail — St. Louis-Los Angeles
- Baggage-dormitory — St. Louis-Fort Worth
- 14-4 sleeper* — St. Louis-Fort Worth
- 10-6 sleeper** — St. Louis-Fort Worth
- Coach, 76 seats — St. Louis-Fort Worth
- Coach, 60 seats — St. Louis-Fort Worth
  (Previous six cars set off at Longview, Texas, for MP *Texas Eagle* No. 21 to Fort Worth; Los Angeles storage mail car continues via MP No. 27 to El Paso to connect with the Southern Pacific)
- Coach, 60 seats — St. Louis-Houston
- Diner-coach — St. Louis-Houston
- 14-4 sleeper — St. Louis-Houston
  (Previous three cars set off at Palestine for MP No. 41 to Houston)
- 10-6 sleeper — St. Louis-Mexico City
  (Continues from San Antonio to Laredo on the MP *Aztec Eagle*, also train No. 1, and from Laredo to Mexico City via the National Ry. of Mexico, NdeM)
- 14-4 sleeper — St. Louis-San Antonio
- Diner-lounge — St. Louis-San Antonio
- Dome coach, 42 seats — St. Louis-San Antonio
- Coach, 72 seats — St. Louis-San Antonio
- Coach, 60 seats — St. Louis-San Antonio
- Coach, 60 seats — Palestine-San Antonio
- 14-4 sleeper — St. Louis-Alexandria, La.
  (Set out at Little Rock, Ark., for MP No. 31 to Alexandria)
- Baggage-express — Little Rock-Texarkana
- Baggage-express — Little Rock-Hope, Ark.

(18 cars St. Louis-Little Rock, 19 cars Little Rock-Hope, 18 cars Hope-Texarkana, 21 cars Texarkana-Longview, 15 cars Longview-Palestine, 10 cars Palestine-San Antonio.)

* 14-4: 14 roomettes and 4 double bedrooms.
** 10-6: 10 roomettes and 6 double bedrooms.

Consist Table 5
Amtrak *Eagle*

Amtrak train 22, the *Eagle* from San Antonio, Texas, approaches Chicago Union Station on October 19, 1981, with an all-Superliner consist behind an F40PH. The *Eagle* name had recently been revived; when first launched in the 1970s, Amtrak's Chicago-San Antonio train was called the *Inter-American. Tom Nelligan photo*

Chicago-St. Louis
Superliner-equipped intercity train, three days a week (from the November 1982 *Model Railroader*, page 96).

- Locomotive, F40PH
- Superliner baggage-coach, 78 seats* (short-distance passengers)
- Superliner baggage-coach, 78 seats (short-distance passengers)
- Superliner diner, 72 seats
- Superliner coach, 77 seats** (long-distance passengers)

(4 cars Chicago-St. Louis)

*Superliner baggage-coach seats 78 on upper level in closely spaced seats and has a large baggage compartment on the lower level.
**Superliner long-distance coach seats 62 on upper level and 15 on lower level in widely spaced leg-rest seats.

Chicago-San Antonio
Superliner-equipped long-distance train, four days a week on a secondary route (from the November 1982 MR, page 96).

- Locomotive, F40PH
- Superliner sleeper***
- Superliner coach, 77 seats (long-distance passengers)
- Superliner diner, 72 seats
- Superliner coach, 77 seats (long-distance passengers)
- Superliner baggage-coach, 78 seats (short-distance passengers)
- Superliner baggage-coach, 78 seats (short-distance passengers)

(6 cars Chicago-San Antonio)

***Sleeper has 14 economy rooms, 5 deluxe rooms, 1 family room, and one handicapped room.

Amtrak uses a few basic types of Superliner cars to assemble a variety of train consists. Modelers can enjoy the same options with assortments of cars like these Kato N scale models. From the left we see a dining car, a Sightseer Lounge car, a long-distance coach, and a sleeping car. *Andy Sperandeo photo*

Consist Table 6
Amtrak *Southwest Chief*, train No. 3, Chicago-Los Angeles

The *Southwest Chief* is Amtrak's Chicago-Los Angeles train on approximately the same route as the old Santa Fe *Chief*. When train 3 arrived at Los Angeles Union Passenger Terminal on June 28, 2005, it had sleeping cars on both ends. Sleeper 32082, *Indiana*, brought up the rear of a consist with matching Superliner IV striping. *Andy Sperandeo photo*

Arriving at Los Angeles (from author's notes of June 28, 2005).

- Locomotives 43 and 19 (coupled "elephant style"), GE P42s
- Baggage car 1250 (ex-Santa Fe ACF smoothside stainless)
- Superliner transition sleeper* 39013
- Superliner sleeping car 32099, *New Mexico*
- Superliner dining car 38006
- Superliner Sightseer Lounge car 33039
- Superliner coach 34035
- Superliner coach 31011
- Superliner coach 34026
- Superliner sleeping car 32082 *Indiana*

(8 cars Chicago-Los Angeles.)

* Sleeper has 14 economy rooms, 5 deluxe rooms, 1 family room, and one handicapped room.

Consist Table 7
Amtrak *Pacific Surfliners* at Los Angeles

Amtrak operates the *Pacific Surfliner* service in partnership with the state of California. Fast, frequent trains run between San Diego and Los Angeles, San Diego and Goleta, and San Diego and San Luis Obispo. This is L.A.-San Diego train 566 ready for boarding at Los Angeles Union Passenger Terminal on June 28, 2005. *Andy Sperandeo photo*

Southbound; northbound consists are the same but with cab car leading; all M-K Amerail double-deck California cars (from author's notes of June 28, 2005).

Train No. 566, Los Angeles-San Diego
- Locomotive 464, Electro-Motive F59PHI
- Pacific Business Class 6852, *Elysian Park* (reserved-seat service including beverages, snacks, and newspapers)
- Coach-cafe 6304
- Coach 6407
- Coach 6452, *Mission Beach*
- Coach-baggage 6951, *Point Loma* (cab car)

(5 cars Los Angeles-San Diego.)

Train No. 768, San Luis Obispo-San Diego
- Locomotive 450, Electro-Motive F59PHI
- Pacific Business Class 6804
- Coach-cafe 6351, *Tecolote Canyon*
- Coach 6410
- Coach 6412
- Coach 6400
- Coach-baggage 6905 (cab car)

(6 cars San Luis Obispo-San Diego.)

◀ The *Pacific Surfliner* weekday service includes two trains in each direction between San Luis Obispo and San Diego, making intermediate stops at Los Angeles Union Passenger Terminal. This is southbound train 768 from S.L.O. departing L.A. on June 28, 2005. The *Surfliners* are push-pull trains, and when this consist returns on a northbound schedule, coach-baggage-cab car 6905 will be leading. *Andy Sperandeo photo*

FIVE
Stations and terminals

The Little Rock, Ark., station on Jay Polk's N scale Missouri Pacific Arkansas Division is a through station like its prototype, with freight main lines bypassing the platform tracks. Little Rock was the scene of much passenger-train switching with connecting trains being split or combined, action that Jay models in his operations. *Bruce Petty photo*

The stations where passenger trains load and unload are vital parts of a passenger railroad's infrastructure. They can also make attractive and operationally interesting models. This chapter will look at the different types of stations and some of their supporting facilities.

By the strictest definitions, a terminal is where a train begins or ends its run, and a station is a place where a train stops along the way. In practice, however, these definitions become blurred. The same facility may be a terminal for one train and a station for another or, if shared by multiple railroads, a terminal for some and a station for others. Nor is there a clear distinction in terms of track layout, since there are examples both of trains originating and terminating at through stations and of stub stations being used by trains passing through a city.

Stub or head stations

In a stub station (illustration, page 71) single-ended stub tracks are arranged alongside passenger platforms. The station building is usually across the end of the tracks, but may be on one side or the other. In large cities, tracks might be below street level or even underground, and in those cases the station building could be above the tracks. Or the station tracks might be elevated above street level, with the terminal building either across the end of the tracks or to one side.

Passenger platforms are typically located between pairs of stub-ended tracks. Some or all track pairs may have "escape crossovers" near their inner ends, allowing arriving engines that have pulled in to uncouple and be released through the crossover while their trains remain standing. In the busiest stub stations there may be a third track between a pair of platform tracks. It functions as an escape track, so that even with arriving trains at the platforms on either side there's still a clear path for releasing their locomotives.

Of course trains don't always head into stub stations. In many cases they turn on a wye track and back in. Or when a stub station is used as a stop along the route of a through train, trains in one direction might head in and back out, while those going the other way would back in and head out.

You might wonder how these sometimes-lengthy backing maneuvers were controlled in the times before radio communications or push-pull operations with m.u. cables through the length of a train. It was done using the conductor's communication whistle and brake valve (photo at bottom right).

The air signal line connected through the train – including pipes beneath box express, express refrigerator, and milk cars – allowed the conductor to signal

Chicago's Dearborn Street Station was a stub station with tracks and platforms at street level. The clock tower of its head house looms in the distance above the peaked roof of the train shed, and umbrella sheds supported by overhead trusses extend to the ends of the platforms. As the Monon *Thoroughbred* departs for Louisville on this late 1940s morning, no fewer than three switch engines are at work. *Harold E. Williams photo*

Inside a stub station: Three yellow-and-brown *Streamliners* are lined up at the bumpers in the Chicago & North Western's North Western Terminal in Chicago in the late 1930s. From left to right are the *City of Denver*, *City of San Francisco*, and *City of Los Angeles*. The C&NW will forward the jointly operated lightweight trains west and hand them off to the Union Pacific at Omaha Union Station. *C&NW Ry. photo*

The last coach on Southern Ry. train 25 is carrying a brake valve extension hose, known in slang terms as a "monkey tail," hooked up to its vestibule gate. The valve on the end of the hose allowed a conductor or brakeman to control the train brakes during backing movements. Train 25 was a local from Atlanta to Columbus, Ga. *Leonard A. McClean photo*

the engineer with an air whistle in the locomotive cab. Standard signals prescribed by the operating rule book told the engineer to go ahead, stop, and back up.

The conductor also controlled the train brakes during backing movements with a brake valve on the last car. This was generally built in on observation cars, but any car could have a brake valve extension, sometimes known as a "monkey tail," connected to its rear train line glad hand and hooked up onto the vestibule tailgate. In addition to hearing signals from the communication whistle, the engineer could see the conductor's brake pipe reductions (brake applications) on the engine's train air pressure gauge and regulate the locomotive accordingly.

There were also stub stations without escape tracks where trains headed in. Locomotives would have to wait in the station until a switcher pulled the train out to the coach yard or to another station track. With diesel operation there were stations where switchers pulled the entire train, locomotive included, out to be serviced in a coach yard.

Through or side stations

In a through station, all or most of the platform tracks are double-ended, so trains pull in at one end and pull out at the other (illustration at right). At busier through stations there will usually be a separate freight line bypassing the station tracks, but at smaller facilities or where less passenger station work is done, freight trains often pass through on main tracks. The station building is typically to one side of the platform tracks, but it may be above them if the tracks are below street level.

Again the usual arrangement is for pairs of tracks to alternate

◀ Here's the Missouri Pacific's through station in Little Rock, Ark., the prototype for Jay Polk's N scale model shown at the start of this chapter. It's 3:50 p.m. on June 15, 1960, as train 220 to Memphis pulls out behind E3 no. 7001. Three other trains are in the station and two switchers are at work. The double-track freight main line curves past the station tracks to the right. *J. Parker Lamb Jr. photo*

Central Station in Memphis, Tenn., shows off its through station layout in this south-facing aerial photo. The station was situated on the Illinois Central's north-south main line, but also served trains of the Chicago, Rock Island & Pacific and the St. Louis-San Francisco. Rock Island and Frisco passenger trains backed into Central Station from the east-west main lines crossing the IC at the top of this view. Note that all the station tracks are elevated above street level, eliminating many grade crossings. *Illinois Central photo*

The Atchison, Topeka & Santa Fe's station in Oklahoma City is seen here from street level. The platform sheds and passenger cars at the left show how the through station's tracks were elevated above the streets, part of a grade-separation project through the city's downtown. The station's concourse extended under the tracks, with ramps leading up to the platforms. Although designed to be architecturally imposing, this station is small enough to be represented on many model railroads. *Santa Fe Ry. photo*

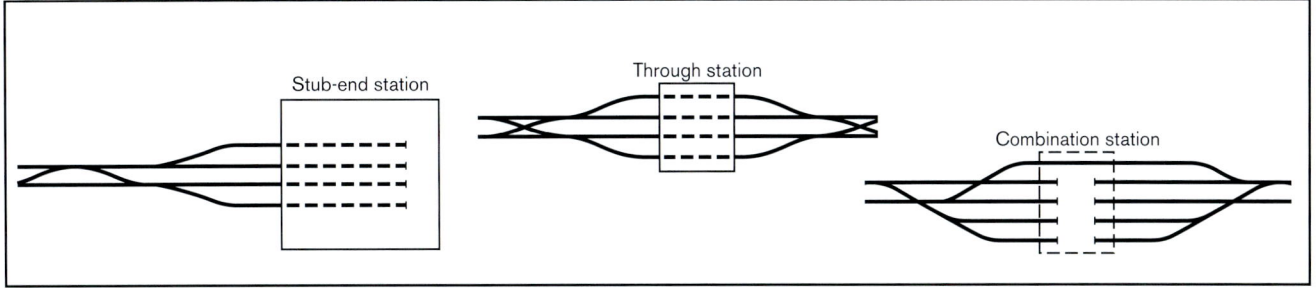

At the south throat of Chicago Union Station, the Great Northern *Empire Builder*, operated by the Chicago, Burlington & Quincy east of the Twin Cities, pulls in past a waiting Burlington switcher for a mid-afternoon arrival in July of 1949. To the right a Pennsylvania RR train is being backed to its platform by its Fairbanks-Morse diesels, while behind it the Pennsy's *General* for New York City waits to depart. The station tracks and platforms are below street level, along the South Branch of the Chicago River. *Bob Lorenz photo*

One of the largest union stations was St. Louis Union Terminal, where trains backed into stub tracks under a giant train shed though a pair of interlaced multi-track wyes. Baltimore & Ohio diesel no. 77 is backing in with arriving train 3, the *Diplomat* from Washington, D.C., in this 1951 image. In the background, blue-and-gray Missouri Pacific head-end cars are being switched by a Baldwin diesel of the Terminal Railroad Association (TRRA) of St. Louis, the station's operator. The two-story brick building at right is the TRRA interlocking tower controlling the extensive complex. *R.S. Plummer photo*

with passenger platforms, but because the tracks are double-ended there's no need for escape tracks. Some adjacent stub tracks may serve terminating local trains, as setout tracks for cars from through trains, and for loading and unloading baggage, mail, and express cars.

In a stub station, passengers can easily reach the train platforms from a concourse or lateral platform across the end of the tracks, but through stations need other arrangements. At smaller, less busy stations or those operating stops where the main concern is servicing the trains, grade-level walkways may suffice to allow passengers to cross tracks going to or from their trains. In busier situations this would be avoided by using a concourse either below or above the tracks.

If the station tracks are below street level, a concourse can extend across them with stairs, ramps, or elevators down to the platforms. These facilities were typically enclosed to protect passengers from the weather and the smoke of passing engines. If the tracks are at or above street level, the concourse can pass below them with stairs, ramps, or elevators up to the platforms. In either case there will still be some need for grade-level crossings between platforms for moving mail, baggage, and express wagons to and from trains on any track.

Just because trains can pass through a through station doesn't mean they always do. Kansas City's Union Station was a through station that served as a terminal for roads such as the Kansas City Southern and the St. Louis-San Francisco. Even the Atchison, Topeka & Santa Fe, whose overland long-distance trains operated through Kansas City, had some trains that originated and terminated there.

Conversely, the joint Union Pacific/Wabash *City of St. Louis* trains operated through Kansas City even though it was a terminal for each of those railroads.

Union stations

A union station is one serving the trains of two or more railroads. In another example of the slippery language describing passenger stations, there are well-known stations that served more than one railroad without the benefit of a "union" in their names. The New York Central's Grand Central Terminal in New York City also served some trains of the New York, New Haven & Hartford, as did its Manhattan neighbor, the Pennsylvania RR's Pennsylvania Station. Chicago's Dearborn Street Station was home to trains of its joint owners, the Chicago & Eastern Illinois, Erie, Grand Trunk Western, and Monon, and also had a big-time passenger railroad as a tenant, the Santa Fe.

"Union station" was often a political term, used to describe a project to consolidate rail traffic from a number of separate railroad depots into a single facility. Usually this promised greater convenience to passengers and gave city governments opportunities for land redevelopment and grade separation schemes. In the first half of the 20th century, when most union station plans were carried out, civic and business leaders also valued the effect of a suitably impressive passenger station as a gateway to their community. The railroad companies didn't always share these priorities, but were generally persuaded to some degree of cooperation.

Union stations could be either stub or through stations. Among the stub stations were Los Angeles Union Passenger Terminal (LAUPT), New Orleans Union Passenger Terminal (NOUPT), St. Louis Union Terminal, and Washington (D.C.) Union Station. Through union stations included Atlanta Union Station, Dallas Union Terminal, Jacksonville (Fla.) Union Terminal, the Kansas City Union Terminal mentioned earlier, Cincinnati Union Terminal, Cleveland Union Terminal, and Omaha Union Station. Whatever the track layout, we can see that "terminal" was the preferred title in most locales, although they all tended to be called "union station" in everyday speech.

Of special interest to modelers, some union stations were related to or controlled by terminal railroads with their own switching power. Examples of these would be the Kansas City Terminal RR at KCUT and the Terminal Railroad Association at St. Louis Union Terminal. In New Orleans the blue-and-orange SW8 switchers were simply lettered with the initials of the station, "NOUPT." In other union stations, switchers were provided by the user railroads, as was the case with the Santa Fe, Southern Pacific, and Union Pacific at LAUPT.

Platforms and train sheds

In most of North America, passenger platforms were and are just slightly above rail level, from 2" to 16" above the top of the rail. The once-familiar metal step box was carried in the vestibules of all passenger cars to assist passengers in reach the car steps from low platforms. Platforms can gently slope to or near rail level where grade-level track crossings are installed for baggage wagons and carmens' vehicles.

The main exceptions to the prevalence of low platforms are in the northeastern United States, where high platforms at car-floor level (about 48" above the top of the rail) are used on commuter lines and in heavily trafficked mainline stations. Both Grand Central Station and Pennsylvania Station in New York City have high-level platforms.

Passenger platforms must be wide enough for the safe passage of both passengers and baggage, mail, and express trucks. According to the historic 1916 text *Passenger Terminals and Trains*, by John Droege, the minimum width for a station platform is 12 feet, with the edge of the platform from 4 feet to 5 feet, 6 inches

These station platforms at Denver Union Station are raised a few inches above railhead height for the convenience of passengers and have concrete umbrella sheds for shelter. (The sides of these sheds were later cut back to give more clearance for dome cars.) The shiny streamliner is the Chicago, Rock Island & Pacific's *Rocky Mountain Rocket*, brand-new in this 1937 view. *Wm. Moedinger Jr. photo*

The Atchison, Topeka & Santa Fe's Barstow, Calif., station has railhead-height platforms between evenly spaced tracks and no shelters. This terminal in the Mojave Desert wasn't a destination for many passengers, but several Santa Fe trains between Chicago and Los Angeles set out and picked up cars at Barstow to make connections to Oakland and the San Francisco Bay Area. The platforms are more for operational than passenger convenience. *Santa Fe Ry. photo*

from the center line of the track. Such minimum platforms require track centers of 20 to 23 feet. For comparison, parallel main tracks may be on 14- to 16-foot centers.

When there are posts on the platforms to support train sheds, greater width is needed, and the same source says that 20 to 24 feet are typical platform widths. That puts track centers into the range of 28 to 34 feet.

Model platforms usually compromise on something less than these widest dimensions, but they will be most convincing if they maintain the 12-foot minimum.

Various kinds of shelters were used to protect passengers from the elements. Nineteenth-century railroads ran tracks directly into and through station buildings. Some New England examples of these stations survived into the 20th century, but rapid growth in the size and length of trains generally made them obsolete. In the late 19th and early 20th centuries, train sheds providing a roof over all platform tracks were used at many stations.

More popular at small to mid-size stations were roofs or sheds over individual platforms, with the tracks between them open to the sky. This pattern was also adopted for the last of the large terminals, including union stations in Cincinnati, Los Angeles, and New Orleans.

In some cases the platform sheds were constructed to partially overhang the tracks, in an effort to shelter passengers as they boarded or alit from trains. Such overhangs at Denver Union Station had to be cut back, however, when the railroads it served began using dome cars.

Station support – the coach yard

Beyond the passenger stations were the supporting coach yards, cleaning tracks, and other facilities. While not often modeled, these do offer opportunities both for layout scenes and operations. The process of getting a train ready for its next trip, known as "turning" because the consist

◀ The Southern Pacific's Mission Road coach yard in Los Angeles has platforms below railhead height for maintenance workers and has pole lines to provide power for lighting and service equipment. The RIP (repair in place) tracks are to the right, where wheelsets and other spare parts are stored outside the maintenance buildings. *Don Sims photo*

This automatic carwasher is cleaning a streamliner as a coach yard switcher slowly pulls the train through the machine. The location isn't specified, but is probably in Texas, as the *Sunbeam* operated between Dallas and Houston on the Southern Pacific's Texas & New Orleans subsidiary. *David P. Morgan Library collection*

A model of an air-brake test cart like this one used by the Chicago & North Western would make an interesting detail for a coach yard. The brake valve, gauges, and air reservoir allow brake operation to be tested on cars and trains not coupled to a locomotive. *C&NW Ry. photo*

Wheel-drop pits like this one at the Chicago & North Western's 40th Street Shops in Chicago allow for quick replacement of worn or damaged wheelsets. Note how the rails on these pit tracks are fastened with clips attached to U-bolts embedded in the concrete walls of the servicing pit. *C&NW Ry. photo*

would be sent back in the opposite direction, took place in the coach yard.

Coach yards usually had storage tracks long enough for entire trains and also had tracks for storing extra and replacement cars. Train consists might remain the same for days or weeks at a time, especially for featured trains and flagship streamliners. However, when traffic required the addition of extra cars, or cars in a train's regular consist had to be sidelined for repairs, the coach yard would draw on its pool of stored cars to make the changes.

Extra cars would also be used to make up additional sections of a scheduled train and for specials and troop trains. Generally the major terminals of a rail system maintained the largest pools of extra cars, with fewer cars available at intermediate points. When it was necessary to originate a special train at a smaller station, cars might be "deadheaded," moved out of service at the head end of regular trains and set out where they were needed. Or an entire "DHQ" (deadhead equipment) train could be assembled and run to where it was needed as a section of a regular schedule or as a passenger extra.

Coach yards also included cleaning tracks where trains could be cleaned both inside and out. These were typically arranged with platforms on either side of each track to give car cleaners access to the sides and windows of both sides of each car. Cleaners would also spruce up the interiors of trains and install freshly laundered headrest covers (known in Pullman service as "tidies").

Cars could be swept out with hand brooms or vacuum cleaners, but some busy coach yards used full-car vacuum systems. These had large suction fans in a housing that fit tightly against the diaphragm at one end of a car. With the vestibule door at the opposite end locked open, the fan would suck out trash from the entire length of the car.

Mechanical car washers were installed at some large terminals for cleaning the exteriors of whole trains. A switcher would couple to the consist to be cleaned and draw it slowly through the car washer's detergent sprays and rotating brushes. In general these machines cleaned only the sides of passengers cars while the roofs, less visible to the public, were left to accumulate locomotive soot, road grime, and other "weathering."

Car washers didn't have a lot of effect on trucks and underbody equipment, either. At least one major railroad, the Atchison, Topeka & Santa Fe, made it a practice to spray fresh silver paint on the trucks and unskirted underbody equipment of cars turned in its coach yards.

Major coach yards usually included commissaries to restock dining and lounge cars, and laundries to supply fresh linens. Where there were many sleeping cars to be serviced, the Pullman Co. maintained its own laundries. Linens were usually exchanged on the cleaning tracks, but dining cars might be switched out of the train consists and spotted at a commissary loading dock. (It wasn't unusual, either, to restock dining and lounge cars in the station tracks while a train was spotted for loading, especially with fresh meats and produce, and with ice for refrigeration.)

Car repairs were also a function of the coach yard. "Running repairs" not requiring a full car shop were performed on RIP (repair-in-place) tracks similar to those in freight yards. At the RIP track, defects in brakes, car heating and air-conditioning, water supply, couplers, and running gear could all be attended to. Using jacks, the RIP crew could replace bearings, wheelsets, and even entire trucks. Of special interest to modelers, these were mostly open-air facilities with everything in plain sight.

Usually major car repair and rebuilding would be handled in a large shop handling all the passenger cars for the entire railroad. The Pullman Co. operated its own car shops at various points across the country to maintain the cars it owned or leased.

Mail, express, and baggage handling

The Post Office, responsible for secure and expeditious handling of mail and parcels, often built facilities adjacent to large passenger stations. If this wasn't a city's main Post Office, it would be one of the most important substations. At the largest terminals, tracks alongside or extending inside the Post Office building allowed for efficient loading and unloading of Railway Post Office and mail storage cars.

At smaller stations mail and parcels were trucked between the station and the Post Office, and cars were most often loaded and unloaded either on the passenger platform tracks or on dedicated tracks adjacent to them. In the smallest online stations these exchanges took place on the passenger platforms while trains were stopped. Of course, the Railway Mail Service was also famous for picking up and delivering mail "on the fly" at the smallest stations where trains didn't stop at all.

Railway Express Agency operations paralleled those of the Post Office, with express buildings similar to large freight houses at the most important terminals. Sealed express cars might be loaded some time before a train's departure and added to the consist after the train was spotted at its passenger platform. Working or messenger express cars might receive packages up to a few minutes before the train left.

When express refrigerator cars carried perishables, they usually were not iced or re-iced at the railroads' icing stations, because those were situated for the convenience of freight trains. The most common method was to ice the cars from trucks equipped with elevated platforms, whether the reefers were spotted on designated express tracks or at the passenger platforms.

Passenger baggage was received in station baggage rooms before departure and loaded into the baggage cars from carts on the passenger platforms shortly before departure. The procedure would be reversed upon arrival. At intermediate stations, it was the responsibility of the train baggage man to unload the proper bags and accept baggage checked by boarding passengers.

Smaller stations

At cities and towns along the line, smaller stations performed most of the same functions as their

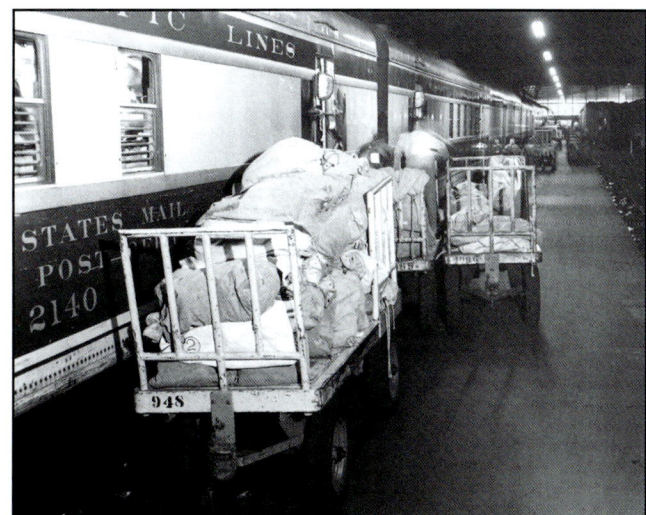

Inside the train shed at St. Louis Union Terminal, postal workers load mail into Railway Post Office cars on Missouri Pacific train 9 on April 22, 1958. This train made an overnight run to Kansas City and handled a lot of mail and express business. A tunnel connected the Post Office and the station, and pneumatic hoists were used as elevators between the tunnel and the platforms. Note the windshields used by RPO clerks picking up mail on the fly. *David P. Morgan Library collection*

Mail and express are unloaded from a Monon passenger train during a stop at an unidentified small-town station. The car to the left is a converted World War II troop kitchen car. Several railroads purchased surplus troop kitchens and troop sleepers after the war at bargain prices and rebuilt them as baggage and express cars. *David P. Morgan Library collection*

The Rock Island's westbound *Choctaw Rocket* to Oklahoma City makes a station stop at McAlester, Okla., in 1949. A worker is pulling a cart laden with mail sacks up to the modernized heavyweight baggage-RPO car. Notice the wooden platform crossing in the foreground and the heavyweight Pullman sleeping car on the connecting St. Louis-San Francisco line. *Robert A. Hadley photo*

At Colorado Springs, the outer platforms were connected to the station by tunnels, with the platform stairways coming up under small brick buildings as on the right-hand platform. This station at the south end of Colorado's Joint Line served trains of the Colorado & Southern (a Burlington subsidiary), the Denver & Rio Grande Western, and the Santa Fe. *A.C. Kalmbach photo*

big-city counterparts on a lesser scale. The station agent was responsible for selling tickets and helping passengers, sometimes with the assistance of ticket clerks, and the agent might or might not have baggage and express handlers to assist with those functions. The Post Office picked up and delivered mail at the station, but the railroad's agent was responsible for sending and receiving mail on stopping and passing trains. In some very small towns the station was also the Post Office, with the agent serving as the postmaster.

Small-town stations typically had a baggage and express room where shipments could be secured while awaiting the arrival of either a train or the express delivery truck. Baggage carts, also used for mail and express, would be stored inside or kept handy on the platform. The mail crane where Railway Post Office cars picked up mail on the move was often at a far end of the platform, away from waiting passengers, and also as far as possible from where train crews picked up clearances and orders from the station's train-order operator.

On a single track line, the passenger platform would most often be alongside the main track. As

At Downer's Grove, Ill., a suburban station on the Burlington's three-track main line from Aurora, Ill., an iron picket fence discourages passengers from crossing tracks in the path of speeding trains. It's July 1946, and a Burlington Pacific is wheeling four cars full of commuters toward Chicago Union Station. *I.E. Griffith photo*

first-class trains in the operating timetable (see the next chapter for more on this), passenger trains were generally entitled to occupy the main line while inferior trains, both scheduled and extra freights, "cleared" for them by pulling into sidings. If a passing siding extended past the station, it often would be on the opposite side of the main so a train on the siding wouldn't block access for passengers, not to mention baggage, mail, and express.

In those situations where a passing siding was between the station and the main line, it was usually long enough so that a freight train could stop to one side or the other and allow access between the station and a stopping passenger train. For obvious safety reasons, operating rules strictly prohibit any other trains from passing between the station and a train receiving or discharging passengers (with the usual rule-book proviso, "unless otherwise provided").

On lines with two or more tracks, underpasses or footbridges allow access between the platforms and the station without the danger of having passengers cross main tracks. Especially at stations handling large numbers of commuters, the railroad might install fences between main tracks to prevent passengers from crossing. On the other hand, stations handling mail, baggage, and express would need track crossings at grade to move carts and wagons across the tracks to platforms on the far side.

Small-town passenger stations are the kind most often represented on model railroads, and they offer great opportunities for close-up detailing. Even when most of the railroad is obviously dedicated to freight service, smaller stations can be focal points for passenger operation.

▶ Union Pacific's *City of Portland* makes a station stop at Green River, Wyo., in July of 1952. Most of the passengers on the platform are through riders stretching their legs while the train is serviced. Notice the service carts on both platforms, the diesel fuel and steam water columns at the far end of the platforms, and another *Streamliner* awaiting its turn. *Richard Steinheimer photo*

▲ This HO scale Dearborn Station diorama was created by brothers Bob and Matt Kosic. The scene captures the characteristic truss-supported umbrella sheds and trains of the Chicago & Eastern Illinois (right) and the Santa Fe, along with a RS-1 switcher of the station's operator, the Chicago & Western Indiana. *Matt Kosic photo*

▶ After dark at Wellington Union Station, a Canadian National express behind 4-8-4 Confederation-type no. 6153 prepares to depart, while the Canadian Pacific's streamlined *Canadian* loads passengers. This impressive station scene is on the O scale Aberfoyle Junction club layout. *Lou Sassi photo*

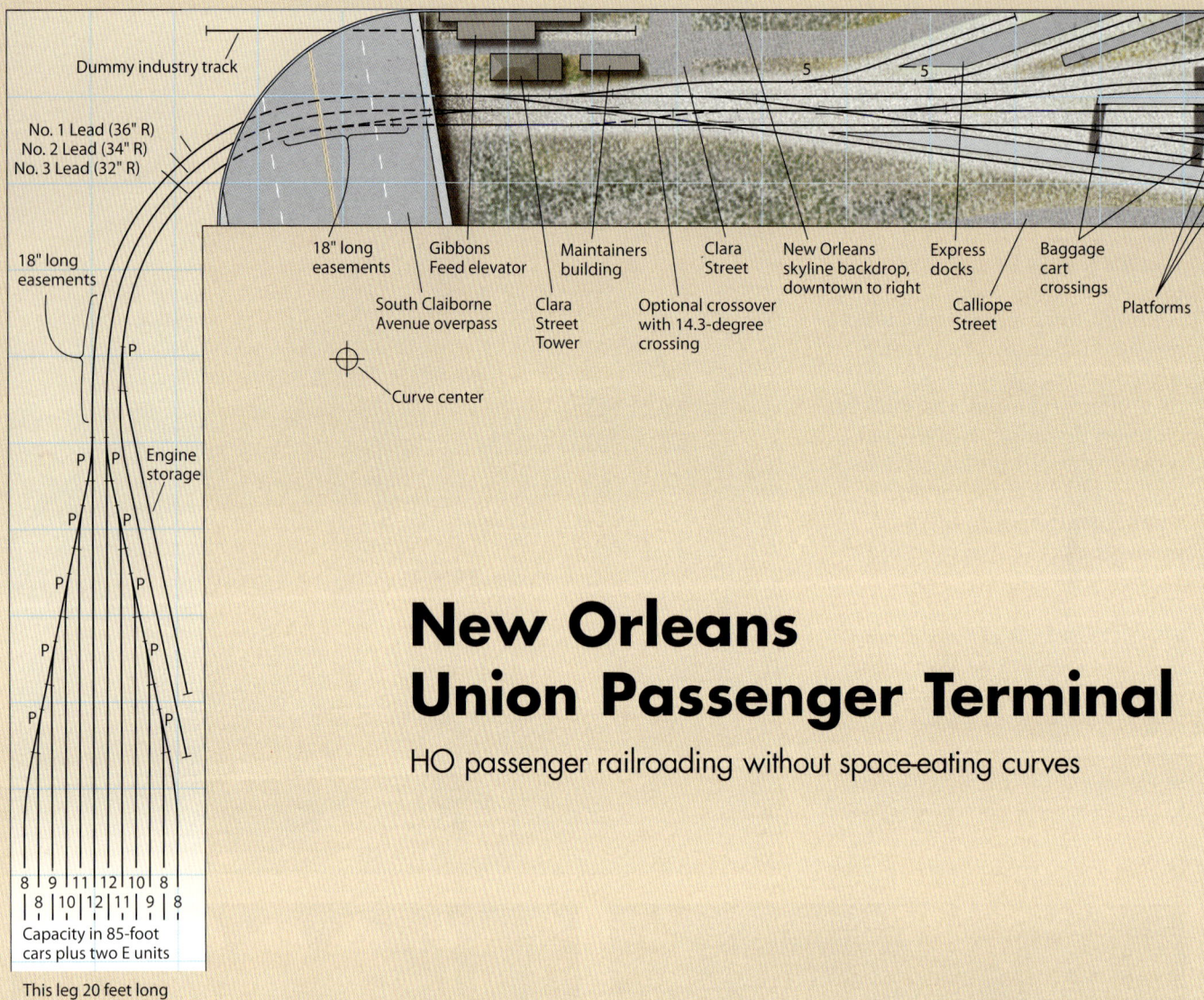

New Orleans Union Passenger Terminal

HO passenger railroading without space-eating curves

What can you do to model passenger train operations in 100 square feet or less? Let's say you like to build or collect detailed HO 1950s streamliner and heavyweight cars, and you want to enjoy them up close in realistic action. The trouble is that for reliable performance you'd like to have curves of at least 32" radius, with easements of course, and relatively gentle no. 8 turnouts. That 100-square-foot limitation doesn't leave a lot of room to swing broad arcs of track. So is it time to switch to Z scale traction modeling?

Prototype to the rescue

Sometimes it's just a matter of picking the right prototype to model, and I've got one to answer the challenges I've posed. When I was growing up in my hometown and wanted to see varied, colorful, big-time passenger railroading, I pedaled my bike (and later drove my mother's car) to a spot at the throat of New Orleans Union Passenger Terminal, right across from Clara Street Tower.

Trains of seven railroads arrived and departed, and for every arrival or departure there was a light engine move to get the power to or from the enginehouse on the "lake" or north side of the South Claiborne Avenue overpass. In between, NOUPT's blue-and-orange SW8s were almost always busy hauling consists out to the coach yard for cleaning and servicing, spotting trains back at the platforms for loading, and switching baggage, mail, and express cars on the tracks to the "downtown" (east) side of the station.

What makes it the perfect prototype for a less-than-100-square-foot layout was that arriving trains turned on a wye out beyond the enginehouse, then backed about a mile and a half into the station's stub-end platform tracks.

The kid across from the tower saw trains backing in and heading out in a setting that readily lends itself to a shelf-type layout. If you don't have to turn the trains around, there's no need to devote much precious layout area to curvature.

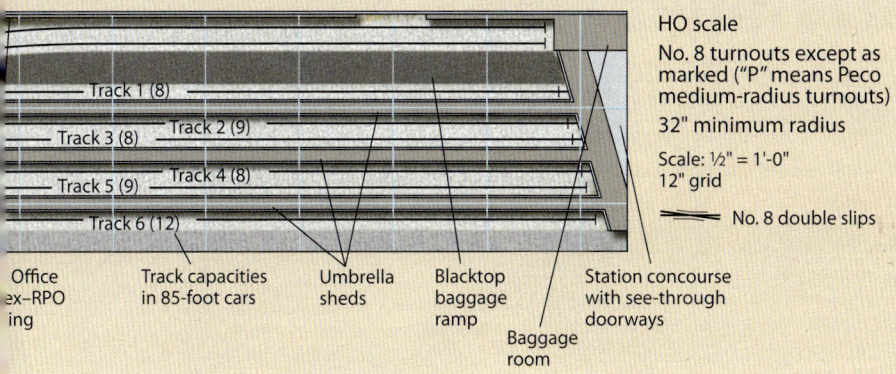

- Track 1 (8)
- Track 2 (9)
- Track 3 (8)
- Track 4 (8)
- Track 5 (9)
- Track 6 (12)
- Office ex-RPO ing
- Track capacities in 85-foot cars
- Umbrella sheds
- Blacktop baggage ramp
- Baggage room
- Station concourse with see-through doorways

HO scale
No. 8 turnouts except as marked ("P" means Peco medium-radius turnouts)
32" minimum radius
Scale: ½" = 1'-0"
12" grid
No. 8 double slips

Peco medium-radius turnouts

Peco's medium-radius code 100 HO turnouts are ideal for staging yards. They are very compact and diverge on a 12-degree angle, a half-degree sharper than a standard no. 5. But unlike standard turnouts, they have a continuous 36"-radius curve through the points, closure rails, and frog.

Because of their sharp angle of divergence, they can form much shorter ladders than conventional turnouts, saving valuable staging track length. Nevertheless, almost all HO locomotives and rolling stock can negotiate their curvature.

It's 4:30 p.m. on a May day in 1954, and the all-sleeping-car *Panama Limited* is leaving New Orleans Union Passenger Terminal on its overnight run to Chicago. Meanwhile, a blue-and-orange NOUPT SW8 is switching express cars by Clara Street Tower. *James G. LaVake photo*

NOUPT on a shelf

This design for an HO scale New Orleans station is an L-shaped layout. The top leg is 22'-6" long and 30" wide, and it represents the station throat and platform tracks on the "river side" (south) of the Claiborne overpass. The left leg is 20 feet long and 28" wide, and it's entirely devoted to a staging yard representing the coach yard, engine terminal, and all the distant cities served by passenger trains from NOUPT. The area is about 78.5 square feet, comfortably within our 100-square-foot target.

The station tracks and throat are compressed of course, with three leads where the real thing had five, and six platform tracks where NOUPT had 12. Still, the general arrangement is pretty close to the prototype, including the extra-long tracks on the "uptown" (west) side of the station. Tracks 11 and 12 were the regular slots for really long trains such as the Southern Pacific's *Sunset Limited* and the Louisville & Nashville's combined *Gulf Wind* and *Pan American* or *Piedmont* and *Crescent Limiteds*.

The mail and express tracks will keep the switchers occupied in between runs to and from the coach yard. On this layout, servicing a train means pulling the recently arrived consist back out to the staging track it came from. The switcher can either wait out there with it or be fiddled (hand-carried) back to the staging throat to reappear from beneath the overpass.

If you had a little more than 100 square feet you could model NOUPT on a U-shaped layout, putting the coach yard and enginehouse across the bottom of the "U." The September 1954 *Trains* Magazine article on NOUPT includes a track diagram that could guide this kind of expansion.

Compact staging ladder

Out in the open, the layout is designed for Walthers code 83 track with no. 8 turnouts and double-slip switches on the station leads and no. 6 and 5 turnouts to handle the shorter head-end cars.

There's no substitute for length in staging long trains, and the Peco medium-radius turnouts described in the sidebar above can save valuable distance. I've tested these with full-length passenger cars close-coupled with Kadee no. 5 couplers and cut-down Walthers diaphragms, and they're completely reliable. (See pages 20-24 in this book for details on the car standards I follow). Even the short S-curves on the two tracks to either side of the center tracks don't cause problems.

Long cars don't look their best going through these tight esses, but my answer to that would be to conceal the staging with storage shelves on top and sliding access doors in front.

With staging capacity for 116 cars in 12 trains, this layout will support a lot of passenger train modeling.

Modeling opportunities

Enjoy multiple prototypes by operating a union station. For the many hobbyists who feel limited by following just one actual railroad, this concept has obvious appeal. If you can find a real station that hosted several of your favorite railroads, you're all set. Or you can model a freelance station that serves the various prototypes you'd like to see under one roof. Another option is to terminate the trains of your freelanced line in a model of an actual union station, including at least some trains of the other railroads. This would have multiple benefits: you'd have a wider scope of passenger trains to model, your terminal operations could be much busier than your line alone might justify, and your freelanced road would gain believability by appearing as an equal alongside recognizable prototype rail lines.

Model the coach yard instead of the terminal. You may find it more space-efficient and operationally interesting to represent a coach yard on your layout instead of the passenger terminal itself. Arriving trains could run past the coach yard into staging tracks playing the part of the terminal, and the coach yard would dispatch a switcher to bring the consist back for servicing. After the coach yard services and rebuilds the train, a switcher moves the consist into staging, from where the train emerges behind a road locomotive for its trip across the modeled portion of the railroad.

One good station may be enough model railroad for the passenger train enthusiast. An extensive depot layout with staging to support a busy schedule of arriving and departing trains would provide a realis-

Special trackwork can help give a model station a big-time atmosphere. This array of double-slip turnouts and scissors crossovers at the south end of Chicago Union Station is something to challenge any model railroad tracklayer. The Burlington Hudson is in charge of a pre-1947 heavyweight *Empire Builder*. David P. Morgan Library collection

tic setting for enjoying and operating your passenger equipment. For an example of this kind of model railroad design, see the sidebar on the New Orleans Union Passenger Terminal layout (page 78). In the next chapter on page 93, John Armstrong's example of the switching interest that could be maintained at a relatively simple through station demonstrates the potential for long-term enjoyment.

Provide realistic eye-level vantage points to get viewers into your station scene. The view along the platforms from inside the head house of a stub station will give views of unexpected realism. If the station tracks can end against a structure flat representing the station, holes in a backdrop or raised fascia will allow looking "through the concourse gates" toward the waiting trains. Inventive modeler Jack Burgess used mirrors to build a periscope into his HO layout that gives operators and visitors a view from the windows of his model of the Yosemite Valley RR's Merced, Calif., station.

Special trackwork gives a station big-time atmosphere. Even a small model terminal with only a few tracks will seem more like a big-city station if it has a scissors crossover or some double-slip switches in its approach tracks. The special trackwork can also conserve layout space and help avoid troublesome reverse curves.

Passenger operations

When model railroaders think and talk about operating their layouts, they most often have freight operations in mind. This is understandable, because carrying freight is the main purpose of most real railroads, and freight traffic offers great variety and opportunities for modelers. Passenger operations, while often overlooked or secondary, can nevertheless offer their own intricacies and enjoyments. Passenger train modelers who devote time and resources to building and acquiring realistic cars and consists will take special pleasure in seeing their equipment put through its paces in a realistic manner.

Paul Dolkos didn't expect his Woodsriver, N.H., passenger station to be a focal point in operations on his HO scale Boston & Maine New Hampshire Division. As the layout's train movements developed, however, the station serves not only B&M trains but also the connecting Canadian Pacific *Alouette* and a mixed train from the shortline Barre & Chelsea. Running the station switcher – here a General Electric 44-tonner – is one of the more popular jobs with Paul's operators.
Paul Dolkos photo

SIX

The significance of time in passenger operations is suggested by the large clock and schedule boards in the concourse of New Orleans Union Passenger Terminal (NOUPT). With 48 scheduled arrivals and departures daily in 1954, punctuality was an important factor in the station's operation. *James G. LaVake photo*

Passengers walking out the NOUPT platforms to board trains such as the Missouri Pacific's *Orleanean* to Houston, Texas, thought of on-time departures and arrivals as an important part of the railroads' service. This MoPac train's last car, by the way, is a through sleeper to Oakland, Calif., by way of the Santa Fe's *California Special* from Houston and *San Francisco Chief* from Clovis, N.M. *James G. LaVake photo*

The importance of time

Timing is important in all aspects of railroad operation, but it takes on special significance when the customers themselves are aboard the trains. Railroads strive to operate trains at times that are both convenient and reliable for these customers (except for some notorious cases in the 1960s when railroad managers tried to discourage travel so they could discontinue unprofitable trains). Speed is important too, and passenger trains generally operate at higher speeds than freight runs, but arriving and departing on schedule is a hallmark of any form of efficient, service-oriented passenger transportation.

Passenger train timing also has importance to the efficiency of freight movements on shared main lines. For this reason, the greatest realism and enjoyment in passenger train operation comes from running trains against timetable schedules. On model railroads this is most often done using "fast" clocks made to run at some speeded-up ratio compared to normal clocks. Faster ratios can compress a greater portion of a day's work on the railroad into an operating session of given length, while slower ratios allow for greater levels of operational detail. Ratios between 2:1 and 6:1 are the most popular.

Superiority of trains

In timetable-and-train order operation, the authority of a train to occupy any given portion of a single-track main line at a particular time is governed by the rules of right, class, and direction (Rule S-71, Standard Code of Operating Rules, March 1949, with "S" indicating a rule applying to single-track main lines). All trains, passenger and freight, must conform to these rules at all times, at the risk of collisions and other dangerous consequences.

The class of any train is designated in the employees' timetable, a document issued to govern the railroad's operations and quite different from the public timetables handed out to travelers. Trains of the first class are superior by rule to trains of the second and third classes, and to extra trains, those operated without timetable schedules (Rule 72). Second-class trains are superior to trains of the third class and to extra trains, and so on. Extra trains, having no timetable schedules and therefore not assigned to any class, have no superiority (Rule 73). The employee timetable also states that trains in a particular direction, most often eastward or northward, are superior to trains of the same class in the opposite direction (Rule S-72).

While class and direction come from the timetable, "right" can only be conferred by train orders issued by the dispatcher, and right is superior to class and direction (Rule 71). The provisions of right give train dispatchers the authority they need to alter and overrule any authority provided by the timetable in the interest of keeping traffic moving both efficiently and safely.

Within the timetable-and-train order regime, passenger trains are always first-class trains. Here the terms "class" and "superiority" have nothing to do with whether a train is the railroad's most luxurious streamliner or a one-coach local making all stops. Both are first class and therefore superior to trains of all lesser classes and to extra trains. Freight trains may be scheduled as second- or third-class trains, or they may operate as extra trains. On some railroads, all freight trains operate as extras, and on some roads second-class schedules are reserved for mixed trains. (There are also a few cases of freight trains operating on first-class schedules for special reasons, but such instances are rare.)

The operational significance of these rules is that inferior trains must always run with respect to the schedules of first-class trains

A Union Pacific freight is in the passing track to meet passenger train No. 1, the westbound *Los Angeles Limited*, in accordance with rules S-71, S-72, and S-89. Inferior trains such as the extra freight operated with respect to the timetable schedules of superior trains like No. 1, so passenger train schedules weren't just important to travelers but also significant in the safe and efficient operation of the railroad. *Fletcher Swan photo*

– passenger trains – and any other superior trains. For trains in the same direction, an inferior train must be clear of the main line – in a siding, yard, or other track – at the time a superior train is due to leave the next station to the rear where time is shown in the timetable (Rule 86).

Regarding trains in opposite directions, an inferior train must be clear of the main line at least five minutes before a superior train's scheduled departure time at that station, except at a scheduled meeting point the inferior train must be clear before the leaving time of the superior train (Rule S-89).

Where yard limits are established, trains or engines may use the main line within yard limits without protecting against other trains, except that they must clear the departure times of first-class trains at the next station where time is shown in the timetable (Rule 93, and note that this rule applies only on main tracks and not on yard tracks or sidings).

These rules establish the priority of first-class trains, both for the safety of passengers and to avoid delays. However, since they require inferior trains to clear not only the first-class trains themselves but also their scheduled times, freight trains can suffer substantial delays when passenger trains aren't running on time.

Timetable schedules remain in effect for 12 hours or until they are fulfilled (Rule 82). Any freight train waiting for a late-running passenger train is required to wait for up to 12 hours after the time shown in the timetable unless a higher authority intervenes.

That authority is the train dispatcher, who under Rule 71 has the power to issue orders changing either the schedule or the superiority of the trains involved. This is what dispatchers do to keep trains moving, and it's a normal part of railroad operations. However, you can see how the operation of all the trains can be simpler, easier, and even safer when the passenger trains stay on their schedules.

Running model passenger trains against a clock brings the full significance of the rules of train movement and the superiority of trains into play, and that's the extra level of drama that passenger trains can bring to even the freight-hauling side of model railroad operations.

On the Southern Ry. double-track main line between Atlanta and Washington, D.C., trains moving with the current of traffic were protected by Automatic Block System (ABS) signals. Trains ran by signal indications. Train 38, the *Crescent* eastbound from Atlanta, could proceed on its schedule as the signals allowed, with signal protection from following trains. *Leonard A. McClean photo*

In Centralized Traffic Control (CTC) territory, as here on the UP across the Mojave Desert, trains operate according to signal indications, which supersede superiority. The CTC dispatcher set remote-controlled turnouts and interlocking signals to put a westbound freight there, allowing eastward train 38, the *Pony Express,* to proceed on its schedule. *Union Switch & Signal Co. photo*

Amtrak trains often operate under Track Warrant Control on hosting railroads. Warrants are issued by computer at the start of a trip or by a dispatcher en route. There's no superiority of trains, and passenger trains depend on dispatchers to run on schedule. Amtrak No. 21, the westbound *Eagle*, was at Tower 55 in Fort Worth, Texas, on May 30, 1984. *Trains magazine photo by J. David Ingles*

When there's no superiority

Other systems of operating authority do without the superiority of trains, but can still recognize the need to move passenger trains on schedule. The principle systems that don't rely on the superiority of trains are:

Current-of-traffic operation with Automatic Block System (ABS) on two or more main tracks.

The simplest case of current-of-traffic operation is a double-track main line with one track designated exclusively for trains moving in one direction and the other track for trains moving the other way. Trains run according to the ABS block signals, whose indications supersede the superiority of trains under the authority of Rule 251 (or D-251, the "D" indicating a rule applying on two or more main tracks).

This system provides safe separation of following trains, but since signals supersede superiority, a passenger train can be delayed by the red or yellow signals behind a slower freight. To allow the passenger trains to stay on schedule, railroads provide sidings at regular intervals so the slower trains can pull off the main line and allow the faster ones to pass. Some roads favor middle sidings, a third track between the two main lines accessible for trains in either direction, while others prefer outside sidings, connecting to only one of the main tracks and used only in the same direction.

Trains can be directed into sidings by "take-siding" signals controlled by a station or tower operator, remotely by the dispatcher, or by interlocking signals operated from lineside towers that also control the siding turnouts. Or trains may be directed to clear the schedules of passenger trains by special "D-251" messages from the dispatcher, which are delivered like train orders by operators at stations or towers along the main line.

One thing you don't normally see in current-of-traffic operation is a train crossing over to the opposite main track to run around a slower train. Part of a current-of-traffic line may have to be operated as single track for emergencies or heavy maintenance, and this can be done by train order authority. However, such movements negate the protection of the one-way signal system and may require temporary train-order offices at remote crossovers, so they aren't used as regular overtaking procedures.

For the most heavily traveled lines, a railroad may use two current-of-traffic tracks in each direction to facilitate frequent overtaking movements. This was the case with the four-track main lines of the New York Central from New York City to Cleveland and the Pennsylvania RR from Gotham to Pittsburgh.

Centralized Traffic Control (CTC) on single or multiple main tracks.

Centralized Traffic Control systems allow a dispatcher or other operator to control turnouts and clear signals over an entire mainline crew district or subdivision. Passing track turnouts and crossovers function in CTC as remote-controlled interlockings protected by absolute signals, with intermediate signals between control points functioning automatically in both directions. The entire system is interlocked to protect both following and opposing movements. Trains are governed by signal indications which under Rule 261 supersede the superiority of trains for both opposing and following movements on the same track.

In CTC territory it's up to the dispatcher to clear the way for the railroad's highest-priority trains, whether they're carrying passengers or freight. With a display on a panel or computer monitors showing the location of every train, the dispatcher has a clear picture of how traffic is flowing and might even calculate that putting a streamliner in a siding for a fast piggyback freight will result in the least possible delay for both trains.

Multiple-track lines in CTC territory usually allow any track to be used in either direction with full signal protection. Dispatchers can set up overtaking moves on parallel main tracks. Lines with three or four main tracks were sometimes reduced to two or three tracks when bi-directional CTC was installed, such was the increased capacity afforded by the flexible control system.

Track Warrant Control (TWC) or Direct Traffic Control (DTC) on single track. Track Warrant Control is the modern equivalent for train orders, which only a few railroads still use. Dispatchers dictate warrants to train crews by radio, telling them to check boxes activating instructions on printed forms and to fill in station names or milepost numbers to define the limits of their authority. Direct Traffic Control is similar except that the railroad is divided into a series of named blocks, and warrants are issued authorizing trains to occupy one or more blocks in sequence. Modern computer automation generates both warrants and checks against issuing conflicting authority.

Again there's no superiority of trains in these systems because there's no authority of any kind except what comes from the dispatcher. As in CTC, the burden of moving passenger trains past other traffic falls on the dispatcher.

Still, schedules and schedule-keeping remain public expectations of a passenger railroad, and companies and public authorities alike strive to meet these expectations. Where Amtrak pays freight railroads to operate its passenger trains on their lines, the freight carriers are paid bonuses for on-time performance.

Building or adapting passenger schedules

Operating model passenger trains without a time schedule can be compared to playing tennis without a net. For realistic effect, model passenger train schedules can be based on the desired departure and arrival times for the markets the trains are supposed to serve. This is best accomplished by following the example of prototype schedules.

If you're modeling a prototype railroad, the logic of following its schedules should be obvious, but it also applies to those operating freelance lines. With your freelanced railroad located on actual maps, you can research the passenger schedules of prototype lines in the same territory for examples of the service it will support. More imaginatively, you might even identify service opportunities that the prototype lines can't or don't exploit, but that your freelanced line is uniquely positioned to develop.

Consider some typical patterns of scheduling. Overnight all-Pullman flyers tended to leave their big-city terminals in late afternoon or evening and operate on timings that would put business travelers into the big city at the other end of the run in time for a productive day after a good night's sleep. This was the timing of the Illinois Central's all-Pullman *Panama Limited* between Chicago and New Orleans, with late afternoon departures and arrivals just after breakfast the next morning.

The IC also operated a fast all-coach streamliner, the *City of New Orleans*, which left both Chicago and New Orleans early each morning. With almost a thousand miles to travel, it didn't arrive at its distant terminal until almost the end of the same day, but it allowed travelers to make the trip without having to sleep overnight in coach seats.

Mail and express trains were often scheduled to depart their terminals several hours after the close of a business day, the better to collect late postings and shipments. These trains typically had long stops built into their timings to load and unload working mail and express cars, and to switch cars in and out at connecting points. Although long and frequent stops lengthened their overall running times, mail and express trains were known for running on fast schedules between stops.

For commuter services, trains are obviously scheduled to bring

Ridin' on the *City of New Orleans*: The southbound side of the Illinois Central streamliner makes its first stop in Kankakee, Ill., after an early-morning dash from Chicago in July 1948. The all-coach train ran on a fast 15-hour, 55-minute schedule to the Crescent City, allowing passengers to reach their destinations without riding overnight. *Herbert R. Heath photo*

people to their jobs in the morning and take them home again in the evening. Usually there are also "shoppers' trains" run during the middle of the day and greatly reduced services on weekends. Equipment used in commuter service generally stands idle between rush periods, and this may require coach yards and other storage tracks both near downtown terminals and in outlying bedroom communities. Some schedules may be arranged primarily to reposition trains after weekends or holidays, or this may be handled by running DHQ extra trains.

Timing and geography

Since a model railroad can only represent a relatively short segment of a passenger train's long run, we need to consider where in such routes our layouts are located when determining how to schedule our trains. On the New Orleans Union Passenger Terminal layout shown at the end of the last chapter, the *Panama Limited* and the *City of New Orleans* could make the arrivals and departures I've described. But if you were modeling the Illinois Central's Memphis, Tenn., passenger station, the *Panama* would pass through in both directions during the hours of darkness, while the *City* would be seen running both ways in daytime.

To look at the western end of one of the big transcontinental systems, the Santa Fe scheduled most of its overland passenger trains for morning arrivals at Los Angeles Union Passenger Terminal, with mostly evening departures. In the June 8, 1947, timetable, five westbounds arrived in the morning, including the *Scout* at 7:15 a.m., the *California Limited* at 7:45 a.m., the Chief at 8:30 a.m., the *Super Chief* or *El Capitan* (on alternate days) at 8:45 a.m., and the *Grand Canyon* at 11:00 a.m. Only the mail and express train, the *Fast Mail Express*, arrived later the same evening, at 8:00 p.m. By that year the *Fast Mail Express* usually didn't carry passengers and wasn't listed in the public timetable. (The *Fast Mail Express* schedules are from the employee timetable of the same date.)

During the day the eastbound departures were limited to *Chief* at 12:30 p.m. and the *Grand Canyon* at 1:30 p.m., but four trains were scheduled to leave the same evening: the *California Limited* at 7:00 p.m., the *Super Chief* or *El Capitan* at 8 p.m., the *Scout* at 8:15 p.m., and the *Fast Mail Express* at 11:30 p.m.

Those timings would be what you'd model on a layout representing the Santa Fe in Southern California, but if you were interested in modeling Santa Fe main lines across New Mexico, the timings would be very different.

Mail and express trains were often scheduled for next-day deliveries at important destinations. This New York Central mail train is pulling out of Toledo, Ohio's Central Union Station at 7:15 p.m. on December 27, 1958. The letters and parcels aboard will reach their recipients in Chicago on the 28th. *Bob Lorenz photo*

At Albuquerque, N.M., the Atchison, Topeka & Santa Fe's No. 17, the *Super Chief*, left, has caught up to a late-running train 19, the *Chief*, at 4:20 p.m. on a spring day in 1946. Seventeen left Chicago seven hours after No. 19 and was scheduled to arrive in Los Angeles an hour and fifteen minutes earlier. *Fred N. Houser photo*

Taking Albuquerque, N.M., as an example, the same 1947 timetable shows a mixture of eastbounds and westbounds scheduled through that station in daylight and early evening hours. This resulted from different trains operating on relatively faster or slower schedules, as well as from having traffic moving through in both directions. Here are the trains scheduled through Albuquerque, showing arrival and departure times for each:

- 1:30, 1:45 a.m., westward *Fast Mail Express*.
- 9:00, 9:10 a.m., eastward *Chief*. 10:35, 10:50 a.m., westward *California Limited*.
- 1:40, 1:50 p.m., westward *Chief*.
- 2:00, 2:10 p.m., eastward *Super Chief* or *El Capitan* (alternate days).
- 4:20, 4:30 p.m., westward *Super Chief* or *El Capitan*.
- 6:15, 6:30 p.m., eastward *California Limited*.
- 9:10, 9:20 p.m., eastward *Fast Mail Express*.

Notice that the *Scout* and *Grand Canyon* trains that came and went at Los Angeles didn't show up in Albuquerque at all. Those trains served the Santa Fe's Southern District between Newton, Kan., and Dalies, N.M. (west of Albuquerque), by way of Wichita, Kan.; Amarillo, Texas; and Belen, N.M.

(The Southern District was the Santa Fe's primary freight route, as it still is for successor BNSF Ry., but it was nevertheless served by two overland passenger trains. Beginning in 1954, the route boasted its own streamliner, the *San Francisco Chief*, running between Chicago and Oakland, Calif., with connecting bus service into its namesake city.)

So where your model railroad is located in terms of the overall system, whether prototype or freelanced, has a great deal to do with both the timings of passenger trains and even which trains

Still steam-powered, although given lightweight streamlined equipment in 1938, the Santa Fe's *Chiefs* meet at Arriba, N.M., during World War II. Eastbound No. 20, right, is on the main line as the train in the superior timetable direction, while westbound No. 19 is in the siding. The trains were scheduled to meet three miles to the west, in Las Vegas, N.M., so 19 is likely about 10 minutes late. *David P. Morgan Library collection*

pass over your modeled main line. Again, freelancers don't have to make up schedules out of whole cloth if they can base timings on those of parallel and supposedly competing prototype railroads.

Train-handling and switching

Smoothness in handling is the goal in running passenger trains. Whether stopping, starting, slowing for a speed restriction, or accelerating from a clear signal, the aim is not to jar passengers out of their seats or knock down anyone moving around in the cars. Not spilling the soup in the diner or the highballs in the lounge car was the mark of a passenger engineer's skill. (However, I've seen experienced waiters on fast passenger trains fill coffee cups only half full, more for the safety and dignity of their customers than for concern about the engineers' reputations.)

Our model trains don't have passengers walking through the aisles or drinking coffee after breakfast, but we can do our best to handle them as if they did. In starting, we can do our best to achieve gentle starts that move every car at once and then accelerate evenly up to running speed after the last car is past the terminal switches.

Prototype engineers often use the technique of working the locomotive against the train brakes, that is, pulling the train up to a station stop with the

Passenger train engineers try to make their movements smooth and steady. They keep in mind that rough handling can spill soup and drinks in dining cars, like this one on the Baltimore & Ohio's streamlined *Columbian*, or even knock down waiters and passengers in the aisles. The same mental image can be useful for engineers of model passenger trains. *B&O photo*

Smooth movements are also the responsibility of passenger station switching crews, like the railroaders assigned to this New York Central U-2f 0-8-0 at the old Union Station in Toledo in August 1940. Gentle handling is always important for safety and comfort, and n*e*ver more so than when switching setout Pullman cars in the middle of the night. *Bob Lorenz photo*

brakes applied on the cars. This keeps the train stretched to avoid any jerky slack action either in stopping or in restarting. Since model trains don't have brakes, we have to simulate, but visually the effect should be of a gentle gliding stop with the cars stopping as the locomotive stops and not bunching up against it.

In fact, passenger cars since the 19th century had buffers, later incorporated into the diaphragms, to control slack action, and the lightweight cars of the late 1930s introduced Tight Lock couplers designed to limit slack in couplings. Like brakes, we generally don't have these features on our models, but in HO scale, at least, I've found that working diaphragms do help to control slack action. The point of controlling slack is to have the train work as a unit, and that's the effect we want to strive for in running our model trains.

Gentleness in switching action is another goal to aim for. When your overnight flyer picks up or sets out a Pullman in the wee hours of the morning, not even sleepers aboard the car being moved should be disturbed, let alone those on the rest of the train. Safety is even more important than comfort, and prototype train and station crews work to switch occupied cars with as little excess motion as possible.

One important technique for gentle switching that's easy to simulate with models is the safety stop. Whenever a locomotive or a locomotive with cars is to couple to an occupied car or train, the engineer will bring it to a complete stop 20 to 25 feet from the coupling. Then, without excess momentum and fully under control, the engine can be eased over that last short gap to couple without moving the standing cars.

In model railroad terms, this coupling technique argues for using electromagnet uncouplers in passenger stations and coach yards. You can make a coupling over an un-energized electromagnet and be confident that the coupler knuckles will close properly. With permanent magnets, the knuckles won't close until the engine pushes them past the magnet, and that's the kind of excess motion we'd like to eliminate in switching passenger trains.

As to whether or not cars are occupied, engine and switching crews always assume any passenger or head-end cars are occupied unless they specifically know otherwise. Even in coach yards, cleaners and maintenance workers may be aboard any car.

Station stops

Once a train is stopped at a station, the best practice is for it to remain stationary until departure time. The train has to be still while passengers get on and off and while baggage, mail, and express are loaded and unloaded. This may seem obvious, but too often model railroad operators don't take the safety of their imagined customers into account.

Where a train stops at a station may be important too. Both head-end cars that will be worked and passenger cars that will discharge and take on riders need to be alongside platforms. In some busy stations, numbered signs were posted on lamp posts and boarding passengers instructed to wait by a particular number to get aboard the proper car. This worked because the train crew would stop the train in exactly the same place every time.

When steam power was still in common use, railroads often located water columns at the ends of station platforms so tenders could be refilled during station stops.

There are cases where so-called "double stops" have to be made because a train is too long or a platform too short, or both. Besides taking extra time, this is a safety risk and requires train crews to let passengers know to stay in their seats, for example,

This Southern Pacific switchman is signaling the engineer of the GS-class locomotive at the left. The 4-8-4 has already stopped a few feet from the cars of its train, the eastbound *Overland*, spotted for loading at Oakland Mole. Now the man on the ground is signaling the engineman, who eases his locomotive back to make a gentle coupling. *Jim Morley photo*

It should be obvious that once stopped at a platform, a passenger train shouldn't be moved while passengers are getting on or off or while mail and express are being worked at the head end. These travelers are boarding the Chicago & North Western's train 153, the *Flambeau 400* from Michigan's Upper Peninsula to Chicago, at Milwaukee on June 2, 1951. Trains *magazine photo by Wallace W. Abbey*

during a first stop to work mail and express cars.

Switching during station stops imposes similar considerations. We can allow a period of time to elapse for passenger handling and only make switching moves after waiting for all riders to be either on or off. Then the road or switch engine crew will work the occupied train with as little extra motion as possible.

When cars are added to and subtracted from a passenger train, air lines and steam pipes or HEP cables have to be disconnected and reconnected. This requires car workers to go between the cars, an extreme safety hazard. Rule 26 provides that when any railroad employee places a blue signal (either a flag or a lamp) at one or both ends of a train, the train may not be moved or coupled to until the blue signal is removed. Only the employee who placed a blue signal is authorized to remove it.

Switching instructions

Some passenger train switching was routine, such as dropping off a setout Pullman or adding cars from a connecting train. These movements were planned and consist information was transmitted to the train conductor at the initial terminal and to intermediate stations where work would be performed. When special movements were required, authorizations would be sent from the railroad's passenger traffic department and again transmitted to conductors and station agents.

In model railroad operation, we can't count on crews knowing their jobs as well as professional railroaders making the same runs every day. To represent the pros' level of execution, experienced layout hosts provide clear, easy-to-follow instructions. There are several effective ways to let your model railroad train and station crews know about switching work to be performed, and you can use the method or methods that work best for the situations on your railroad. Here are a few options:

Train instruction cards. You can provide instructions detailing the operation of each train, including regular pickups and setouts. It also helps to specify station stops to supplement an operating timetable.

Switch lists. Just as for freight service, you can prepare a written list for each passenger train showing the cars in its consist and any pickups and setouts to be

While carmen are inspecting a train or making air, steam, or electrical connections between cars, they protect themselves by marking the train with blue flags at each end of the consist. Standard rule 26 states that a train or other equipment can't be moved or coupled to when so marked. A metal blue flag is hung on the rear car of the UP's westbound *City of St. Louis* while the train is serviced at Rawlins, Wyo., on March 14, 1954. *R.S. Plummer photo*

A carman "laces 'em up" – connects brake and signal air hoses and train steam lines – at New Orleans Union Passenger Terminal. The Alco diesel of the Southern Pacific's subsidiary Texas & New Orleans has coupled to an SP express boxcar at the head end of the westbound *Argonaut* to Los Angeles. *James G. LaVake photo*

made. Or the train may start out with a listing only of its initial consist and find prepared lists at stations where work will be done.

Station schedules. Where a station switcher will be on duty, you can provide a schedule detailing not only when trains are due to arrive and depart, but also any work to be done. This may include specific car identifications and tracks where setouts should be left and where pickups will be assembled.

Car cards and waybills. If your railroad uses car cards with waybills for freight traffic, it can be convenient to adapt the same system for passenger train operations. Most waybills in a train might indicate through movement to the train's terminal, but waybill destinations along the train's route will tell crews where setout cars should be dropped off. Crews can also be instructed to check card pockets for passenger station tracks to find cars to be picked up. Since most pickups will be meant for particular trains, the waybill can include the train number. See Bill Darnaby's article listed under "Further Reading and References" for an adaptation of the car-card-and-waybill system to passenger terminal operations.

Messages. Especially on model railroads using written train orders, out-of-the ordinary movements can be conveyed by message from the dispatcher. Usually these would be delivered at the train's starting point along with its initial clearance card and any train orders, but could also be delivered en route in the same manner as train orders addressed through an intermediate station.

One place I wouldn't recommend placing switching instructions is in your employee operating timetable. This information is rarely found in these documents on the prototype.

Only the railroad employee who placed a blue flag on a train or other equipment has the authority to remove it. This car inspector at Los Angeles Union Passenger Terminal is taking down the blue flag he had hung on the locomotive of UP train 38, the *Pony Express*, signifying that he has completed his work and is no longer under or between the cars. The eastward train was preparing to depart for Ogden, Utah, in February 1953. Trains *magazine photo by Wallace W. Abbey*

A Reading Co. Camelback 4-6-0 leads a commuter train through the industrial outskirts of Philadelphia on Jerry Strangarity's HO scale railroad. Commuter operations are characterized by closely spaced trains running on tight schedules. *Lou Sassi photo*

Modeling opportunities

Add variety to station switching by assigning switchers on limited shifts. During the hours when a station switcher is on duty, the road locomotive will stand by or move out of the way and let the switcher do the work. But at times when the station switcher is off duty, the train crew will have to do any work required with the road engine. In such cases, setouts may simply be left on the most convenient adjacent track for the switcher crew to spot in their next shift.

Build your railroad's schedule by starting with the first-class trains. Even if you're modeling a line that's primarily freight-oriented, you'll get extra realism into your operating plan by developing schedules based on the markets served by your passenger trains and their timings across the mainline segment that you model. You may even find it easier to then draw up freight schedules because you won't be working in a vacuum, and you'll see schedule "windows" when way freights and other trains with online switching to do can get their work done.

Develop schedule contrasts to emphasize the roles of different passenger trains. Your railroad's long-distance streamliner may speed across your main line making few or no stops, and then your local or accomodation train will be defined by the many stops it makes to serve small communities. An all-chair-car economy train may leave your terminal station early in the morning to complete its trip by late evening, while an overnight train with sleeping cars will pull out in the late afternoon for a next-morning arrival.

A New York Central engineer switches head-end cars at the station in Troy, N.Y. The key to efficiently switching through trains is having the cars that are to be handled lined up in advance. *Jim Shaughnessy photo*

Get online switching done on schedule by means of advance planning. The twin requirements of safety and comfort mean that station switching should be done at a deliberate pace, so the keys to getting work done on time are to be prepared and eliminate wasted motion. The station switcher can arrange cars to be picked up in proper order and spot them in a convenient location before the through train's scheduled arrival. Cars to be set out can be carried at the front or rear of the through train's consist, or at least grouped together, to keep the breaks in the train's order to a minimum. The switcher's schedule of work or instructions can specify where the cars to be handled will be in the arriving train. If trains have work to do on the front and rear during one stop, assign two switchers to work both ends simultaneously.

Practice smooth train-handling techniques. Working to give your imaginary passengers the safest and most comfortable ride you can will add interest to even the simplest through passenger run, and it will add to the impression of realism created by your carefully modeled trains. Of course, to achieve this you'll have to maintain high mechanical and electrical standards for your rolling stock and trackwork. Then everything will run better, not only the passenger trains.

On-line passenger train switching

In his landmark book, *Track Planning for Realistic Operation* (Kalmbach Books), John Armstrong created this example of the switching operations that might go on at a mid-point passenger station. This would be a good concept for a small layout built around a single passenger station or could be incorporated as one focal point on a larger layout. The station layout is simple, but quite a lot can be done with it. The key to making it work would be staging tracks arranged to keep the trains coming.

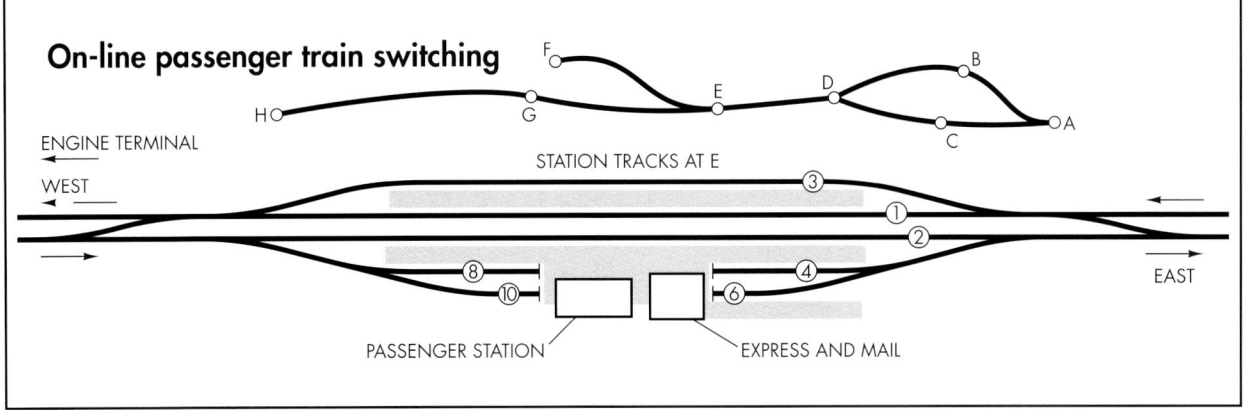

Station timetable at "E"

Note: no passenger switching crew on duty 12:01 a.m. to 8:00 a.m.

Train No.	Direction	Designation	From	To	Via	Arrive "E"	Leave "E"	Switching at "E"
41	West	"F" Night Express	A	F	B	2:25 a.m.	2:40 a.m.	Road engine picks up express and storage mail cars for "F" from track 8; set out express car from "A" on 8.
26	East	Night Limited	H	A	B	4:52 a.m.	5:15 a.m.	Road engine cut off while train remains on track 2 and head-end traffic is worked; run around train via track 1; pick up diner from 3, set on rear of train. Return to head end via 1, set out express car from "H" on track 6.
27	West	"G" Night Express	A	G	C	6:45 a.m.	6:59 a.m.	Road engine picks up diner-lounge from track 3; place in train ahead of coaches and sleeper. (Sleeper continues to "G.")
102	East	Local	E	A	B	–	7:30 a.m.	Road engine comes from engine terminal one hour ahead of departure time via track 2, picks up express car off No. 26 from 6, RPO from 4, and couples to coach on 3 to make up train there.
52	East	Day Express	F	E	–	9:38 a.m.	9:58 a.m.	No. 52 in on track 2 with RPO, coach, diner-lounge; road engine to engine terminal via track 1. Switcher pulls diner-lounge from rear of train and sets out on 8; picks up parlor car on 10 and sets on No. 52's through coach on 2, and awaits arrival of No. 32 via crossover onto track 1.
32	East	Day Express	G	A	C	9:44 a.m.	9:58 a.m.	Switcher pulls rear sleepers of No. 32 through crossover to 2, picks up parlor and coach, and sets whole cut back onto No. 32, which leaves for "A" via east crossover. Switcher sets RPO from No. 52 on 3.
31	West	Day Express	A	G	C	2:46 p.m.	3:02 p.m.	Reverse operations from those consolidating Nos. 52 and 32; switcher makes runaround move to set parlor car on 10 after No. 31 clears. Engine from No. 52 may haul No. 51.
51	West	Day Express	E	F	–		3:06 p.m.	
28	East	Evening Express	G	A	C	5:45 p.m.	5:48 p.m.	Number 28 drops sleeper deadheaded from "G." Switcher parks this sleeper on track 8, ready for occupancy at 10 p.m.
101	West	Local	A	E	B	10:15 p.m.	–	Terminates; road engine to engine terminal. Switcher places deadhead diner-lounge (dropped at "D" by No. 28) on track 8, coach on 3, RPO on 6, baggage-express cars on 3.
25	West	Night Limited	A	H	C	10:46 p.m.	11:05 p.m.	Road engine cuts off. Switcher sets baggage-express cars from No. 101 onto No. 25, runs around via track 2, sets out diner from No. 25 on 2. After departure of No. 25, switcher sets diner on track 8, takes diner and diner-lounge from 8 and sets out at the west end of track 3.
40	East	Night Express	F	A	C	11:40 p.m.	11:55 p.m.	Road engine cuts off. Switcher sets sleeper from track 8 on rear, runs around via track 1 and picks up express car from track 4 and sets on No. 40.

Further reading and references

Books:

Armstrong, John, *Track Planning for Realistic Operation, Third Edition*, Kalmbach Books, 1998

Droege, John, *Passenger Terminals and Trains*, Kalmbach Books, 1969 (republication of a 1916 original)

Drury, George H., *Guide to North American Steam Locomotives*, Kalmbach Books, 1993

_____, *The Historical Guide to North American Railroads, Second Edition*, Kalmbach Books, 2000

Dubin, Arthur D., *More Classic Trains*, Kalmbach Books, 1974

_____, *Pullman Paint and Lettering Notebook*, Kalmbach Books, 1997

_____, *Some Classic Trains*, Kalmbach Books, 1964

Frailey, Fred W., *A Quarter Century of Santa Fe Consists*, RPC Publications, 1974 (available on CD-ROM from the Santa Fe Ry. Historical & Modeling Society at www.atsfrr.net)

_____, *Twilight of the Great Trains*, Kalmbach Books, 1998

Johnston, Bob, and Welsh, Joe, with Schafer, Mike, *The Art of the Streamliner*, MetroBooks, 2001.

Long, Bryant A., with Dennis, Wm. J., *Mail By Rail*, Simmons-Boardman Publishing Corp., 1951

Maiken, Peter T., *Night Trains, The Pullman System in the Golden Years of American Rail Travel*, Lakme Press, 1989

Marre, Louis A., *The Contemporary Diesel Spotter's Guide, Second Edition*, Kalmbach Books, 1995

_____, *Diesel Locomotives: The First Fifty Years*, Kalmbach Books, 1995

McDonnell, Greg, *Field Guide to Modern Diesel Locomotives*, Kalmbach Books, 2002

Passenger Car Catalog: Pullman Operated Equipment 1912-1949, Kratville Publications, 1968

Randall, W. David, *The Official Pullman-Standard Library, Selected Heavyweight Cars*, RPC Publications Inc., 1995

Roseman, V.S., *Model Railroading's Guide to Railway Express Agency*, Rocky Mountain Publishing Inc., 1992

Ryan, Dennis, and Shine, Joseph, *Southern Pacific Passenger Trains, Vol. 1 – Night Trains of the Coast Line*, Four Ways West, 1986

Stegmaier, Harry Jr., *Baltimore & Ohio Passenger Service, 1945-1971, Vol. 1, The Route of the National Limited*, TLC Publishing, 1993

Welsh, Joseph, *Passenger Trains of Yesteryear: Chicago Eastbound*, Kalmbach Books, 2002

_____, *Passenger Trains of Yesteryear: Chicago Westbound*, Kalmbach Books, 2002

_____, *Pennsy Streamliners: The Blue Ribbon Fleet*, Kalmbach Books, 1999

_____, and Howes, Bill, *Travel by Pullman, a Century of Service*, MBI Publishing Co., 2004

White, John H. Jr., *The American Railroad Passenger Car*, Johns Hopkins University Press, 1978

Zimmerman, Karl, *Domeliners: Yesterday's Trains of Tomorrow*, Kalmbach Books, 1998

Periodical articles:
(from *Model Railroader* magazine unless otherwise named)

Chapman, Bob, "Kitbashing B&O's *National Limited*: Part 1," March 2002, pages 58-63

_____, "Kitbashing B&O's *National Limited*: Part 2," April 2002, pages 91-100

Darnaby, Bill, "Card-order operation for passenger trains," October 1993, pages 74-77

_____, "Kitbashing heavyweight Pullman cars – Part 1," April 1989, pages 106-113

_____, "Kitbashing heavyweight Pullman cars – Part 2," May 1989, pages 104-113

_____, "Kitbashing streamlined passenger cars," March 1994, pages 80-87

_____, "Paint Shop: Pullman two-tone gray," May 1989, pages 119-121

Dolkos, Paul J., "Building wood [passenger] cars from styrene," May 2001, pages 82-84

_____, "Passenger cars from core kits, Part 1: Get the cars you want by combining unique sides with common carbodies," March 1995, pages 56-61

_____, "Passenger cars from core kits, Part 2: Two different approaches to working with etched-metal car sides in HO and N scale," April 1995, pages 72-78

Ellison, Frank, "Passenger train operation," June 1951, pages 8-13

Grivno, Cody, "Amtrak's mail and express fleet," March 2003, pages 71-73

Hediger, Jim, "A railroad service you can model – Auto-Train," December 1974, pages 46-53

_____, "Amtrak at 20," June 1991, pages 82-91

_____, "Amtrak's Superliners," November 1982, pages 84-97

_____, "Auto-Train car interiors," January 1975, pages 60-63

_____, "Troop kitchen cars," February 2002, page 80

Hitchcock, Chuck, "Twelve hours at Argentine," *Model Railroad Planning*, 1997, pages 10-17

Kennedy, W. Gibson, "Build a complete Kettle Valley passenger train," June 1959, pages 26-32, with drawings on pages 38-41

_____, "Building a head-end car from photos and basic dimensions," August 1960, pages 46-50

_____, "Car for the silk express," February 1965, pages 42-46

_____, "Plush for your passengers – build an observation car," September 1966, pages 34-40

Kohlmann, Keith, "Realistic stainless steel," July 2003, pages 94-95

Larson, Paul, "Gems of passenger train operation," April 1958, pages 50-55

_____, and Odegard, Gordon, "MR rides a doodlebug," April 1959, pages 24-30, with track plan on page 53

McGuirk, Marty, "Troop sleepers," December 2001, page 88

Morin, Jim, "Modeling Northern Pacific trains 57 and 58," October 1987, pages 72-76

Odegard, Gordon, "Building passenger cars of the 1890s," December 1970, pages 51, 54-56, with drawings on pages 46-50

_____, "More cars of the 1890s – diner, parlor, sleeper," June 1971, pages 43-49

_____, "Pike sized steam and diesel passenger trains, October 1989, pages 77-80

Schafer, Mike, "Modeling the *Asheville Special*," January 1981, pages 94-96

_____, "Pike-sized passenger trains," November 1980, pages 66-69

_____, "Pike-sized passenger trains: Part 2," January 1981, pages 90-93

Sebastian-Coleman, George, "Amtrak Viewliners," January 1997, pages 104-106 and 115-116

Shaffer, Frank E., "Passenger station operations," September 2005, pages 62-68

Scott, Dick, "Building an O scale Brill [gas-electric] car," July 1998, pages 98-108

_____, "Styrene to streamliner," January 2004, pages 86-91

Sperandeo, Andy, "8 pike-size passenger trains," May 2003, pages 48-53

_____, "Kansas City Southern trains 9 and 10," November 1980, pages 70-72

_____, "The 1947 *Empire Builder*," December 1991, pages 108-123

_____, "Pike-size steam passenger trains," October 1987, pages 77-79

_____, "Toledo's Central Union Terminal, HO layout design for a passenger train fan," February 2003, pages 74-77

Wider, Pat, "BR&BS Express Refrigerator Cars," *Railway Prototype Cyclopedia 7* (2002), pages 1-77

_____, "Express Boxcars – Addendum," *Railway Prototype Cyclopedia 8* (2003), pages 1-27

_____, "Express Refrigerator Cars – Addendum," *Railway Prototype Cyclopedia 9* (2003), pages 61-86

_____, "The Fast Ones: BX Express Boxcars," *Railway Prototype Cyclopedia 6* (2001), pages 2-39

_____, "Modeling Plan 3410 12-1 Pullman Cars – Part One," *Railway Prototype Cyclopedia 1* (1997), pages 37-47

_____, "Modeling Plan 3410 12-1 Pullman Cars – Part Two," *Railway Prototype Cyclopedia 2* (1998), pages 23-47

_____, "Modeling Pullman Heavyweight Passenger Cars – Part Three: The Most Common Cars," *Railway Prototype Cyclopedia 3* (1999), pages 78-83

_____, "Production WWII Troop Sleeping and Kitchen Cars," *Railway Prototype Cyclopedia 5* (2000), pages 25-41

_____, "Six Lightweight Sleeping Cars: Prototypes for the Walthers HO Scale Streamline Car Models," *Railway Prototype Cyclopedia 11* (2005), pages 1-113

Web sites:

Madden, Thomas C., The Pullman Project, www.pullmanproject.com

Sandifer, J. Steven, Steam Ejector Air Conditioning, www.trainweb.org/jssand/SEAC/Index%20Overview?SEACOver.htm

Spear, D. Garrett, Pullman Truck Information, prr.railfan.net/passenger/GSPEAR/GSPEAR_Pullman_Trucks.htm

Webber, Bob, et al, Lightweight Car Model Spreadsheet, passenger.drgw.org/PassHome.htm

Manufacturers and suppliers

Alclad II
501 S. Falkenburg Rd., No. D-68, Tampa, FL 33619
Phone: 813-643-1232
Web: www.alclad2.com
Products: Chrome lacquer for stainless steel finish

American Limited Models
Box 7803, Fremont, CA 94537-7803
Phone: 510-796-6593
Fax: 510-794-8488
E-mail: bob@americanlimitedmodels.com
Web: www.americanlimitedmodels.com
Products: HO and N scale diaphragms for passenger cars and diesel locomotives, N scale passenger car core kits

American Models
10087 Colonial Industrial Dr., South Lyon, MI 48178
Phone: 248-437-6800
Fax: 248-437-9454
E-mail: info@americanmodels.com
Web: www.americanmodels.com
Products: S scale passenger cars, passenger car parts and trucks, and locomotives

American Model Builders/Laserkit
1420 Hanley Industrial Ct., St. Louis, MO 63144
Phone: 314-968-3076
Fax: 314-968-0799
E-mail: laserkit@aol.com
Web: www.laserkit.com
Products: HO and N laser-cut acrylic passenger car sides and passenger car detail parts

Athabasca Scale Models Ltd.
200, 1316 9th Ave. S.E., Calgary, Alberta, Canada T2G 0T3
Phone: 403-250-7719
Toll-free orders: 877-247-7719
Fax: 403-250-7303
Web: www.athabascashops.com
Products: HO and N scale passenger car kits, detail parts, and storage boxes

Athearn Trains
1550 Glenn Curtiss St., Carson, CA 90746
Phone: 310-763-7140
Fax: 310-763-7449
Web: www.athearn.com
Products: HO and N scale passenger train cars and locomotives

Bachmann Industries
1400 E. Erie Ave., Philadelphia, PA 19124
Phone: 215-533-1600
Fax: 215-744-4699
E-mail: sales@bachmanntrains.com
Web: www.bachmanntrains.com
Products: HO, N, On2½, and large scale passenger cars and locomotives

Bethlehem Car Works
P.O. Box 325, Telford, PA 18969
Phone: 215-721-3006
Fax: 215-723-2542
E-mail: jgreene@netcarrier.com
Products: HO passenger car kits, detail parts, and trucks

Branchline Trains
333 Park Ave., East Hartford, CT 06108
Phone: 800-289-4000
Web: www.branchline-trains.com
Products: HO passenger car kits, detail parts, and trucks

Brass Car Sides
715 S. 7th St., St. Peter, MN 56082-1435
Phone: 507-931-2784
E-mail: dchenry@gac.edu
Web: www.brasscarsides.com
Products: HO and N scale etched-brass passenger car sides, car kits, and parts

Broadway Limited Imports
601 Shenandoah Village Dr., Ste. 9E, Waynesboro, VA 22980
Phone: 540-949-8300
Fax: 540-949-8377
E-mail: info@broadway-limited.com
Web: www.broadway-limited.com
Products: HO passenger cars and locomotives

Centralia Car Shops
1468 Lee St., Des Plaines, IL 60018
Phone: 847-297-2118
Web: www.desplaineshobbies.com
Products: HO and N scale passenger car kits

The Coach Yard
Box 593, Del Mar, CA 92014-0593
Phone: 626-796-7566
Fax: 626-796-7566
E-mail: carman@thecoachyard.com
Web: www.thecoachyard.com
Products: HO imported brass passenger cars and trains, trucks, parts, and power trucks

Con-Cor International
8101 E. Research Ct., Tucson, AZ 85710
Phone: 520-721-8939
Fax: 520-721-8940
Web: www.all-railroads.com
Products: HO and N passenger cars and trains

D&G Models
Box 641364, Los Angeles, CA 90064-1364
Phone: 310-452-7993
Products: HO type 43-R (triple bolster) passenger trucks

Eastern Car Works
Box L624, Langhorne, PA 19047
Phone: 215-757-4448
Fax: 215-757-4448
Products: HO passenger car kits, parts, and trucks

Eastern Seaboard Models Corp.
Box 316, Little Ferry, NJ 07463-0316
Web: www.esmc.com
Products: N scale passenger car sides for American Models core kits, and passenger car kits with etched brass sides

Fine N Scale
5306 Sunset Ave., Anacortes, WA 98221
Phone: 360-299-4527
E-mail: info@finenscale.com
Web: www.finenscale.com
Products: N scale cast resin passenger train and express car kits

Funaro & Camerlengo/ Funaro Scale Models
10 Funaro Ct., Honesdale, PA 18431
Phone: 570-224-4989
E-mail: fandc@ezacess.net
Web: www.fandckits.com
Products: HO molded resin passenger car kits

Great Western Passenger Car Details
Box 414, Unit 35, 2855 Pembina Hwy., Winnipeg, Manitoba, Canada R3T 2H5
Products: HO passenger car detail parts

InterMountain Railway Co.
Box 8502-0839, Longmont, CO 80501
Phone: 303-772-1901
Fax: 303-772-8534
E-mail: intermountain@intermountain-railway.com
Web: www.intermountain-railway.com
Products: HO and N assembled passenger cars from Bethlehem Car Works, Centralia Car Shops, and Train Station Products kits; HO passenger car wheelsets

JJL Models
733 Seymour Rd., Bear, DE 19701
Products: HO Delaware, Lackawanna & Western diner and tavern-lounge kits

JnJ Trains
Box 683, Pleasantville, IA 50225
Web: www.jnjtrains.com
Products: N scale passenger car sides and details

Kadee Quality Products Co.
673 Ave. C, White City, OR 97503-1078
Phone: 541-826-3883
E-mail: mail@kadee.com
Web: www.kadee.com
Products: HO, S, O, and large scale couplers; HO passenger-car wheelsets

Kato USA
100 Remington Rd., Schaumburg, IL 60173
Phone: 847-781-9500, ex. 209
Fax: 847-781-9570
E-mail: erich@katousa.com
Web: www.katousa.com
Products: HO and N passenger cars and trains, locomotives

Keil-Line Products
6440 McCullon Lake Rd., Wonder Lake, IL 60097
Fax: 815-728-0595
E-mail: oscaler@aol.com
Products: O scale passenger car interior kits and passenger truck kits

La Belle Woodworking Co.
5101 Ridge Rd., Cheyenne, WY 82009
Phone: 301-433-9909
Fax: 301-433-9949
E-mail: infor@labellemodels.com
Web: www.labellemodels.com
Products: HO, HOn3, and O scale wood passenger car kits

Laser Horizons
1529 16th St. NE, Canton, OH 44705
Products: HO ABS plastic passenger car sides

M&R Car Sides
N Scale Supply, 5024 Kipling St., Wheat Ridge, CO 80033
Phone: 303-456-6702
Fax: 303-456-5479
E-mail: sales@nscalesupply.com
Web: www.nscalesupply.com
Products: N scale etched brass passenger car sides, detail parts

Micro-Trains Line
351 Rogue River Pkwy., Box 1200, Talent, OR 97540-1200
Phone: 541-535-1755
Fax: 541-535-1932
Web: www.micro-trains.com
Products: N scale troop sleepers and kitchen cars, couplers, coupler conversions, passenger trucks, and wheelsets

MTH Electric Trains
7020 Columbia Gateway Dr., Columbia, MD 21046
Phone: 410-381-2580
Fax: 410-381-6122
Web: www.mthtrains.com
Products: O scale passenger cars and locomotives

New England Rail Service
Box 40, Newbury, VT 05051
Phone: 802-866-9020
E-mail: info@newenglandrail.com
Web: www.newenglandrail.com
Products: HO conversion and detail parts for Rivarossi heavyweight Pullmans and other heavyweight cars

NKP Car Co.
1260 Lake St., Hanover Park, IL 60133
Phone: 630-289-4800
E-mail: bnsf7@aol.com
Web: www.nkpcarco.com
Products: HO and N etched brass passenger car sides and car kits

Overland Models
3803 W. Kilgore Ave., Muncie, IN 47304
Phone: 765-289-4257
Fax: 765-289-6013
E-mail: info@overlandmodels.com
Web: www.overlandmodels.com
Products: HO, N, and O scale imported brass passenger cars and locomotives

Palace Car Co.
Box 973, Kearny, NE 68848-0973
Phone: 308-238-5099
E-mail: info@palacecarco.com
Web: www.palacecarco.com
Products: HO and N scale passenger car interior kits and interior detail parts

Precision Scale Co.
3961 Hwy. 93 N, Box 278, Stevensville, MT 59870
Phone: 406-777-5071
Fax: 406-777-5074
Web: www.precisionscaleco.com
Products: HO and O scale imported brass passenger cars, cast brass and plastic passenger car details parts, trucks, and wheelsets

Railway Classics
Box 22011, Eagan, MN 55122
Phone: 314-846-4391
Fax: 952-997-2712
E-mail: sales@railwayclassics.com
Web: www.railwayclassics.com
Products: HO and N scale imported brass passenger cars and trains, locomotives

Rapido Trains Inc.
140 Applewood Crescent, Concord, Ontario, Canada L4K 4E2
Phone: 905-738-6445
Fax: 905-738-6265
Web: www.rapidotrains.com
Products: HO passenger cars and passenger trains

Reboxx Inc.
7 Kane Industrial Dr., Hudson, MA 01749
Phone: 800-935-2195
Fax: 978-568-9942
E-mail: infor@reboxx.com
Web: www.reboxx.com
Products: HO passenger car wheelsets, foam-lined storage boxes

Red Caboose
Box 250, Mead, CO 80542
Phone: 970-535-4601
Fax: 970-535-4521
E-mail: stacktalk@aol.com
Web: www.red-caboose.com
Products: HO and N X-29 box express car kits

Red Cap Line
Box 6457, Burbank, CA 91510
Phone: 818-362-5313
Products: HO passenger car interior detail parts and lighting kits

Santa Fe Ry. Historical & Modeling Society
1205 S. Air Depot, No. 101, Midwest City, OK 73110-4807
Phone: 405-732-3562
Fax: 800-507-4142
E-mail: sfrhandms@mindspring.com
Web: atsfrr.net
Products: HO Santa Fe etched brass passenger car sides and car kits

Sunshine Models
Box 4997, Springfield, MO 65808-4997
Products: HO molded resin express boxcar and express refrigerator car kits

Train Station Products
Box 360, Granville, OH 43023
Phone: 740-587-0684
Fax: 740-587-4182
Products: HO passenger car kits, core kits, detail parts, and trucks

Union Station Products
2264 Sutherland Dr., Memphis, TN 38119
Phone: 901-277-4237
Web: www.unionstationproducts.com
Products: HO and N scale styrene passenger car sides, ready-to-run passenger cars by custom order

Walthers Trains
Box 3039, Milwaukee, WI 53201-3039
Phone: 414-527-0770
Fax: 414-527-4423
E-mail: sales@walthers.com
Web: www.walthers.com
Products: HO passenger cars, lighting kits, parts, and trucks

Weaver Models
Box 231, Northumberland, PA 17867
Phone: 570-473-9434
Fax: 570-471-3293
E-mail: qcweaver@ptd.net
Web: www.weavermodels.com
Products: O scale passenger cars, troop sleepers and kitchen cars, and locomotives

Wheels of Time
Box 846, Mountain View, CA 94042-0846
Web: www.wheelsotime.com
Products: N scale ready-to-run passenger cars and urethane resin passenger car kits